Poetry Ireland Review 132

Eagarthóir / Editor
COLETTE BRYCE

Poetry Ireland CLG/Éigse Éireann CTR gratefully acknowledges the assistance of
The Arts Council/An Chomhairle Ealaíon and The Arts Council of Northern Ireland.

LOTTERY FUNDED

Poetry Ireland invites individuals and commercial organisations to become
Patrons of Poetry Ireland. For more details, please contact:
Anne Hendrick, Development Manager,
Poetry Ireland, 11 Parnell Square East,
Dublin 1, Ireland
or telephone +353 1 6789815; e-mail development@poetryireland.ie

FOUNDING PARTNERS
Adrian Brinkerhoff Poetry Fund of the **Sidney E Frank Foundation**
University College Cork

POETRY PATRONS: LYRIC
Joseph Hassett, Marie Heaney, Thomas Dillon Redshaw, Ronan Reid

POETRY PATRONS: SONNET
**Marie Baker, Patricia Ferguson, Alan W Gray, Eithne Hand, Neville Keery,
R John McBratney, Joan McBreen, Marian Richardson**

POETRY PATRONS: STANZA
**Martina Dalton, Emer Foley, Robert Haughton, Isabel Healy, Monica McInerney,
Mary O'Donnell**

POETRY PATRONS: HAIKU
**Sarah Bannan, Amanda Bell, Peter Clarke, Kevin Conroy, Richard Halperin,
Karen Hanratty, Christine Dwyer Hickey, Mary Jeffrey, John D Kelly, Susie Kennelly,
Karen Meenan, Oliver Mooney, Jean O'Brien, Eilín de Paor, Gillian Perdue,
Andy Pollak, John Prebble, Grace Smith, Anne Tannam, Siún Tobin, Jesko Zimmerman**

ISBN: 978-1-902121-84-0   ISSN: 0332-2998

IRISH-LANGUAGE EDITOR: **Aifric Mac Aodha**

PUBLICATIONS MANAGER: **Paul Lenehan** with **Eoin Rogers**, and with the assistance of
Orla Higgins
COVER DESIGN: **Alistair Keady** (**www.hexhibit.com**)
COVER CREDIT: *Over Heavy Seas*, by **Kathy Tynan**

Contents

Editorial

At a recent online poetry event, the poet's mouth very slowly disappeared through the bottom of the screen, leaving only the eyes – a slippage of the phone or whichever device relayed their virtual appearance. This year, in the absence of communal gatherings, poets have ventured gamely, and in some cases reluctantly, into the online sphere. We've positioned ourselves in unforgiving light, loomed absurdly towards the small eyes of laptops, framed in the questionable décor of our living rooms, or the multi-coloured tumult of our bookshelves. Since events have entered the domestic space, it's even possible to cook in the company of poets, as they read to us live from New York or Galway on a screen propped up on the kitchen scales. Or we've Zoom-attended, in speaker-view, our face in one of the tiny boxes bordering the poet's performance. Those of us less acclimatised to the virtual sphere have been gently prodded out of our comfort zones and into the twenty-first century.

How odd it is to miss the poetry reading, the gathering in person from time to time to listen to an author speak aloud their words. And stranger perhaps that such a simple, fairly unchanging format has endured for so long. "Aren't the persuasions of poetry private?" the American poet Kay Ryan once asked. "The right sized room to hear poetry is my head, the words speaking from the page". This year, with the ongoing Covid restrictions, the perfectly-sized venue of our own heads is overdue an airing. The social connection fostered by live events, allowing for the meeting of minds, has been a significant loss. The cause of our disconnection, lest we forget, is that breath – so integral to the poetic endeavour – is temporarily dangerous.

Breath has been much on our minds as we've looped the strings of face-masks around our ears and steered clear of confined spaces. We've noticed anew the pale breath-clouds of others in the freezing air. Paula Meehan, a mesmeric performer of her work, has spoken of the primacy of breath to the poetic line, of the speech act to the art: "Physically to make a poem is to shape breath in space. The text is the record of that". In this issue, she takes a look back along the roads that have led to the milestone of her new *Selected Poems*.

The poem as breath-map, utterance – or more specifically, the imitation of an utterance – makes its performance by the author as fitting a destination as the page. Ailbhe Darcy considers documentary poetry, and – as if in sympathy with our confinement – takes us to two pre-lockdown performances, where body, voice, and text intersect in fascinating ways. Emily S Cooper explores a personal connection with another charismatic performer, the late Irish-American poet Michael Donaghy. Like Meehan,

Donaghy held his attention to craft and performance in equal balance. Speaking his poems word-perfectly from memory, he seemed to inhabit the rhythms of the lines, his expressive hands reminiscent of the great Jacques Brel. Cooper notes the unreality of listening to online recordings of the poet, his living voice not only through the window of a screen but, indeed, of time and mortality.

The online event has its limits, of course, yet manages to harness at least some semblance of the buzz of its physical equivalent. And we're grateful for it, and to the tireless directors who have adapted and 'teched up' their programmes this year. While we await the return of poetic proximity, of the breaths and coughs and greetings in a room, the smells of damp coats and municipal wine, perhaps the journal may also serve as a useful, particle-free meeting place. One aspect of being published in a magazine is the unexpected connection with the other poets in that space at that particular time. The small venue of the journal empties and refills issue by issue: the chairs are stacked and reset, glasses are rinsed, as an ever-widening community of poets comes and goes. We welcome you to this winter gathering.

– Colette Bryce

Denise Riley

1948

i

Your past can't tell it *is* the past.
How to convince it that it's done with, now?
The only touches that I got before I reached eighteen were blows.
It never crossed my mind to look for others' kindness, later on.
But my pigheaded will alone propelled me to my sorrows.

ii

When I could step into the shockingly open world
I wasn't sure of where I ended, or where someone else began.
This was a joyous state.
Under my skin I might have been a man, a kindly one.
Longing leaped in flames, it raced and crackled.
Small winds tore through it, keening
and fanning its chase.
It made the truest of songs –
it was the truth ablaze,
it was pure wanting, bloodied and radiant.
Holy, holy, sang that pursuit
and holier the infants born of it.
Then unholy the contempt that circled me.

iii

Time did, but did not, pass
in muted work and stabs of gaiety
to build some way for us to live
clear of the glaring, yet repeated, risks
of coupledom warped by rancour.
A darling can turn wolfish.

iv

I wished, half-helpfully, to be unseen
or run a website for the hard-to-place
with me as its founder member.
Now I'll brandish my rosy face around
teasing my pratfalls of a baffled need
while hope deferred still hollows me out,
takes clownish leaps about my gouged-out shell.

v

As there's dark humour in a darker time
so there's resilience in an obvious rhyme.

Self-parody deflates a plaintive mime
to make it truer – just *as* pantomime.

vi

The mothers are long dead,
the several fathers too.
What took place is done, though
it murmurs on in you
who got through it alive, with
a bit more extracting to do.

vii

On blackened streets the taint was scoured from doorsteps.
The illegitimate sent off to the infertile,
their pasts expunged, their names altered.
Their records sealed.
No need to mention any of it again.
That was only for the best, it was all for the best.
Everyone meant it for the best.

viii

This present-past hangs on. It says:
'Days flocked with frighteners – they'll circle round you still
though they're long dead who daily clouted you across the mouth –
disgusting animal, you're asking for it, useless object, you want a good thrashing.
You didn't, but you got it anyway, with other things far better not
to get (though, decades later, getting pregnant saved your life
since you did get lovable children). Slaps smelled of bleach
striping your face in wheals each the width of the finger
that made them – you prayed that they'd fade before school.
A knee to the small of your back shoved you down
if you paused on the stairs: *you're bad – bad, through and through.*
You spend your next sixty-eight years working out how far that's true.
So what are you asking for now? To not still hear
these utterances, in the only mother tongue you knew:
*obey without question, you want a real beating, spare the rod
spoil the child, shut your gob or I'll shut it for you
you're neither use nor ornament, you're not like other girls
you don't deserve to be loved, you belong in the loony bin
a child has to have its spirit broken, hold your tongue
you disobedient animal, no one would ever believe you*
– Well, no. Though you'd never expected them to.
Who would have heard you then, who would,
since no one could see how you'd tried to be good.
You can't try any harder than ever you could.'

ix

'That couldn't have happened, you seem so normal.'
– I am so normal. And it did.
Just as it did to thousands.

x

I tell my past it's passed, though it can't tell.
More training, to teach obedience: the toddler
who'd wet herself gripped by the scruff of her neck
and her nose rubbed in it, in freshly damp white cotton.
Their real beloved dog I envied, while I stayed an 'it'
burrowing through straw quills in the kennel
to study the grace of the dog, to poach the secret of being liked.
Yet gradually my life as an 'it' has grown muscular.
Almost, I am that dog.

xi

I won't blame those enslaved by their own rages,
fearful of a baby that would never feel like theirs
yet couldn't be returned to the agency.
I blame the powers that packed us off to them
as misconceived children to be conformed –
easy mishaps in small border towns,
stains on their working families.

xii

Cast to the winds, some might find safe landings,
but others blew onto steel shards.
'Bad blood' was how our bad fortunes described us.
It could all have worked out fine – bar the tick
of a chancy official biro, handing you straight
to the care of gloved anger, or respectable angry anxiety.
But that was the luck of it, that was how it fell out
for surplus postwar children.
The indifferently falling rains of them.

xiii

'More care would get taken in re-homing a dog.'
Though the dog might at least have its pedigree.

Hit and miss (literally) where you ended up.
And each person involved was unknowing.

xiv

This history's too commonplace to tell.
It is a story which so many own.
How do I get it right, alone?
The point of telling is to crack its spell.

xv

'The point of telling is to crack its spell'?
What if it underscores dead violence
as calligraphy – a sentence
maybe freeing, but only if 'done well'?
And when the casual judgements fly
around each teller: 'She's damaged, TMI'?
– Judgment runs everywhere in our material.

Felicity Sheehy

AFTER THE FUNERAL

I rode trains for long mornings
in the autumn light, stunned
at the substance of things:
the dense boots of working men,
the orange spark of tickets.
I sat in window seats
with my hat in my hands,
my face unspoiled in the glass,
flickering over county lines,
over country homes and stables.
Incredible were the women
who sat close by: one knitting
a scarf in thin yellow stripes,
another holding a screen,
and so lit from beneath, as if
by a candle. I watched a man
cut his nails with the precision
of a priest, lining the slim moons
across vinyl seats. And the look
of the whole world, just beyond
the trackline: the children
standing in mapled shadows;
their mothers, smoothing their coats.
I'd watch these little scenes
for what seemed like hours, perfect
in their glassy frames, moving
through like a rainfall
or the deep note of a bell.
When the train stopped
in a clatter of workday sound,
I would try to hold them there
a while longer. But they were
like anything glimpsed
for a second from a silver tunnel
and fixed in the dark hour
of the mind: clearer at a distance,
clearer, now, in passing.

Ian Duhig

THE NAMES OF THE PLAGUE
after the Middle English

The blame gamer, the ill-shamer,
the brave-killer, the grave-filler,
the buck-passer, the eye-glasser,
the sight-saver, the night raver,
the faith-shaker, the rule-breaker,
the duff ruler, the bluff fooler,
the world-beater, the word-eater,
the first aider, the worst-paider,
the spit-sailor, the inhaler,
the high fever, the deep griever,
the dry cougher, the hat-doffer,
the cold creeper, the old-reaper,
the youth-wrecker, the truth checker,
the head-cracker, the lost tracker,
the host-racer, the slow tracer,
the job-loser, the lost boozer,
the cramped-homer, the spread coma,
the room slayer, the doomsayer,
the sick-tricker, the nit-picker,
the mad chatter, the foil-hatter,
the mask-hater, the nurse-baiter,
the flock fleecer, the palm greaser,
the deal-lander, the back-hander
the wrong richer, the song hitcher,
the rhyme rider, the time bider.

(Its chief name is Legion.)

Ian Duhig

SIGHT UNSEEN

Tea bags were the death of tasseographers.
I consulted one of the last here at a fair;
she offered me an Earl Grey or Darjeeling,
saying their big leaves are best for old eyes.

While it was brewing, she shared biscuits
and memories of the Second World War,
reassuring wives, mothers and daughters
behind the blackouts of news and curtains.

It was about comfort even when the news
turned out to be bad. Nobody came back
to moan "I only wish I'd suffered longer!"
Even when she knew, she said, she'd lie.

She told me not to dunk my shortbread,
then to swirl my cup thrice widdershins,
left-handedly; turn it over and then back.
She looked in, paused, and smiled kindly.

Ian Duhig

I wonder what does the old phrase 'the Black Irish' mean now?
Will it still summon ghosts of dark aspect from the lost Armada?
asked one organiser of the Mixed Race Irish Families exhibition
whose own more successful launch I attend from Leeds, online.

I think about the black in my surname and of my nephew's skin;
then, because he shared his surname with my first English home,
pause over Pablo Paddington, acrobat and equestrian for circuses
like Pablo Fanque's, of *Sgt. Pepper's Lonely Hearts Club Band*.

The *Leeds Intelligencer* renders Paddington the 'Flying African'
while the *Manchester Courier* styles him as the 'Flying Indian'
(later, the 'Brazilian Phenomenon'); Cooke's 'Flying Peruvian'
(like the bear) becomes the *Leeds Patriot*'s 'Siamese Aeronaut'.

York's *Herald* carries a stranger tale from a city poorhouse inmate,
Ellen Lowther, fellow circus performer of colour, revealing Pablo
to be female, *so dextrously disguised that he deceived Miss King,*
also an equestrienne of Mr Cooke's circus, till scandal whispered …

A novel story. Pablo's real first name was Joseph, like my brother:
his brother Father George John Paddington, was ordained in Haiti,
another small colonial island marked by an independent disposition,
where their father, George, met their mother, bringing her to Ireland.

I wonder did she, whose name I still search for, bring a magic dowry
and teach it there as ringmistress to her holy, flying, various children?
I think of her while passing Pablo Fanque's Leeds grave, of her son,
Joseph, at Vicar's Croft, the old equestrian arena, where he so entranced.

Lianne O'Hara

DESIGN

you be the boy who was bullied in school
making faces in the snow with / nosebleeds
hurt less when it's cold

i am the silence
          you remember

ripped into you like the holes
in new jeans / you see

fragments of expired youth
                    you

say this is not important
          i am a man

               now

wipe that blood off your mouth

Lianne O'Hara

CAVITIES

I remember a path no one walked. This is where stones were buried, hems covered in autumn mud, where disposable camera images were torn in threes. Underdeveloped. This is where we put secrets in our mouths after seeing a film about four girls in Goth outfits and I am forever the girl with raven hair, the film's penultimate scene star on a hospital bed staring at a faraway sky.

The rule of three does not apply. A sister in crime since the age of five becomes a model at sixteen and her smile moves continents. My father is as proud as her own and forgets I am his daughter for a while. I spit out my secrets on the path and circle the trees for an entire afternoon, but I don't remember where.

When in the same year I adopt a different name I pretend it's inspired by the platinum blonde junkie girlfriend of a punk icon, but really it was always the raven haired girl with a mouth too big for her face. Her mouth intimidates me, its teeth and her eyes all gone wild. She will be remembered by her mouth. This is my first mistake.

I badly want to live in this mouth and forget I am anyone's daughter because what else can you do when you're snorting cocaine off a ledge in a public bathroom stall with a man thrice your age, who says I don't know what I'm doing I could be your father for god's sake. What was your name again, sweetheart.

John Challis

NIGHT CHANGE

I step across the moon,
the small hand

of the clock,
to lay the bundle

of my daughter down,
knowing where

the flooring waits
to exhale.

Night remembers
other nights.

I alight from one life
into another,

from my long
and sobering walk

and creak down
to my knees,

a father, still a child
bowing

to repay his debt.

John Challis

WHERE THE DEVIL GETS IN

All present and correct: the parcels of mown ground,
ruled lines of hedges, rectangles of ploughed mud,
scraggy fringes of silver birches dangling over fences,
their buds right-angled to accommodate the lorries.

But a sense of our bare selves lurks in the soil
and rises when it rains, the ground as bloated as a man
pulled from the river. Drains empty the understreet
and run along the kerb: new streams to be named

should they stay the course and widen over driveways
and welcome mats, and the country become a filter
for poor taste and bad vibes drawn from the groundwater,
stagnating on the green and pleasant lawns.

Natalie Linh Bolderston

NEEDLES, A HISTORY

> *Có công mài sắt có ngày nên kim.* | *Persistence grinds iron into needles.*
> – Vietnamese proverb

i. *1987*

It is snowing the first time
she sews up a boy's leg.

After her shift, she waits for her bus,
tries not to show her face.

A man stops his car, asks her to get in.
She walks away quickly.

The moon gives no more light
than a discarded sharp.

ii. *1975*

When soldiers seized the jewellery shop in Bạc Liêu,
her parents opened a second shop in Saigon
that sold only clocks and sewing needles.

For weeks she stitched gold chains
into the hems of her blouses
while needles ticked.

iii. *1962*

When she was six,
her mother held a metal point over a flame
and punctured her earlobes.

On her knees, surrounded by ice
she bled all summer.

iv. *1972*

One spring, she accepted a vitamin injection
from her pharmacist uncle
after months of eating too little.

It became easy: skin pinched at the hip,
the pop and sigh of a syringe
and hardly any blood. The pain was over
in less than one breath.

Later, for the first time that year,
shadows unpeeled from the walls
and clotted between her legs.

v. *2018*

One winter, she learns
that a rift in the knee is a kind of loss.
She refuses the steroid injection.

Thousands of miles away,
Bà Cố is kept alive with needles
and three prayers a day.

Towards the end, she opens one eye
and takes the hand of someone
she almost recognises.

vi. *1979*

Another winter, she sews coats
for weathers she has never known.

Fake fur gathers in her lap.
The white factory lights miss nothing.

You are not quick enough.
Her mother kisses her bruised fingers.

She bites her cheek,
presses harder on the pedal.

Katie Donovan

TWO WOMEN, ONE GRAVE

Now, at last,
she wants to see his grave.

This is our first time
meeting: she turns out
to be small, straight-nosed,
determined –
oddly familiar.

It was she who ended it,
their long engagement;
moved on, to a better job,
a certainty she needed –
more than what he had to give.

As I puppet my way
through the narrative
of his illness, she grows still.
It is a long drive to the grave,
and I wait
while she has her tears.

I'd like to blame her
for something.
She'd like to pour balm on me.
She thinks quietly –
I imagine –
of her lucky escape.
I think of his misery.

But we are alive now,
and he has been gone
for seven years.

So I drive more hours
and we speak of our children,
as women do:
we women,
who live
long enough.

Katie Donovan

THE THREE WHO WERE LOST

I was the first who stayed alive.
Like some painted over canvas:
the consolation prize.
Then, at last,
a boy, big and bonny
and full of smiles.

He and I carry on
into middle age,
while she still dreams
of the three who were lost.
She has travelled, searched;
adopted others
to assuage her need.

I had my two with ease.
None of her terror,
wondering *can they breathe?*

She never said a word –
except once, when I complained
my son could not latch on,
drew blood
as he gummed fiercely
at my breast.

Be grateful for what you have
she told me.
Her voice was very hard.

Kayo Chingonyi

1. ZERO

1920, nine years before Nellie
is born, a ghost note in simian blood
is loosed by a novice butcher's unsteady
knife-work. Rubies scattering in the mud.
Making a fist she raises it up
to stem the flow and marvel as it slows;
a haemoglobin beck under her toes.

A decade or more before the penny
drops; this blood-punter already abroad
(the names of the dead will always be heavy
as a colony of ants drinking from a gourd).
Men who love men sup on the freedom to love
each other; step together out of clothes
after dancing in clubs that never close.

2. MIGUEL

After dancing in clubs that never close
his allegiance is to a Hammond B3
that, if you play it right, will disclose,
by sympathetic magic of its stuck key,
the traces of a blacker melody.

After church he plays the devil's music,
fingers tap a boogie-speckled blues riff
in praise of fingertips brushing a nose,
deliberate, a darkened corner's hungry
trysts, hips scoring the music's crescendos.

Accustomed to underlay, the seedy
sides of town, he favours bars whose heady
mix of high and low he finds therapeutic
(acquaintance with the night has its uses).

3. ERYKAH

Acquaintance with the night has its uses
in life given over to capital,
its envoys, the trade-offs it produces.
All we build to sublimate animal
selves. She knows this like she knows this hospital –
bedpan by soiled bedpan. Where she meets Miguel,

here to see a friend from forty deuces's
alternate marketplace; call him Confucius.
Mid-smoke he tests his latest philosophical
premise, claims free will is impossible,
every confidence trickster has a tell;
the nucleus of an infected cell.

4. VIRAL

The nucleus of an infected cell
is a pathogen's ultimate gateway –
after the breach, the sounding of a knell,
the ending of a life, or so they say.
I believed it, too, to my great shame,
as did my mother who refused the pills
that would have her here among us still.

The lobby of a Shoreditch hotel,
Miguel is now our ageing DJ
holding the headphone to his ear like a shell
living after so much death, a cliché
of his times that taught him to live day to day.
The dancers heave and swell, in search of thrills,
like droplets moistening a windowsill.

5. RESULTS

Like droplets moistening a windowsill
is how you might, if you were so inclined,
describe nervous energy's overspill
into panic. Waiting for the call, you find
monolithic tombstones occupy your mind;
recalling ads from the decade of Thatcher
that passed judgement and prophesied rapture.

All clear. Sat in bed you cry until
streetlights glance the lattice of the blinds,
your heart a boulder rolling down a hill,
your optimism toughened to a rind
effective, if a little unrefined.
And though, for now, you're spared the hereafter
there are depths of fear no words can capture.

6. SURVIVOR'S GUILT

There are depths of fear no words can capture.
What to do, having been granted reprieve,
with what remains of your life? What if, after
the storm has passed the pasture is relieved
of its fertility? And who to thank for all that you achieve,
given time to work on your vocation,
what spectres attend the celebration?

For all the outward signs you manufacture
pointing to wellness, the stages you complete,
running through the middle there's this fracture.
Each living moment carries a receipt —
as doubting is the price of your belief.
May god bless this blood-borne innovation
sired somewhere in the Congo Basin.

7. ORIGIN MYTH

Sired somewhere in the Congo basin
yet how it grew to populate the earth
teaching us the story of mutation
is the story that attends the very birth
of our kind, the tenuous nature of our worth.
Is it any wonder the road seems so unsteady?
Millions lost to veering paths already.

For those who came before me, a libation!
I conjure you as though we sat around a hearth
when I walk it's your shadow I'm chasing.
Next to my skin I still carry the hurt
finely woven as a cambric shirt
from before akashishi took so many:
1920, nine years before Nellie.

Note: The Bemba phrase 'Bamalwele ya akashishi' means 'Those
who suffer from the germ / virus'

Siobhán Campbell

THE TASTE OF TIME

Martin Malone, *The Unreturning* (Shoestring Press, 2019), £10.
Miriam Gamble, *What Planet* (Bloodaxe Books, 2019), £9.95.
Gerry Murphy, *The Humours of Nothingness* (Dedalus Press, 2020), €12.50.
Julia Copus, *Girlhood* (Faber & Faber, 2019), £14.99 hb.

Martin Malone's third collection, *The Unreturning*, is a deeply serious, yet playful, meditation on the current zeitgeist, our collective myth-making and its very real consequences. The title may refer to the Wilfred Owen poem or it may refer to *The Unreturning Army*, Huntly Gordon's memoir of Flanders which details experiences of the battlefield that seem almost inconceivable to us now. But Malone seems to imply that the battlefield has always been that of our collective consciousness, or more to the point, our propensity to accept the 'given' story along received hierarchies of power. Throughout, there's a tension between the world-weary and the elegiac, between a modern ennui (which he skewers with punchy satire) and an echo of longing for the transcendent moment which, he seems to imply, is the provenance of art, but only of an art which is socially engaged. The reader is to be wary of the misuse of history and of poetry, of 'The eye' that 'seeks out pattern and is satisfied' ('Archives').

It is a book of two halves. 'Ghosts of the Vortex' presents lyrics, written with great authority, and interested in the line, the stanza, and in striking phrasing which inks itself into the brain. We are to understand our responsibility to recognise 'trench honesties / occluded by one century / and the paradigms of myth'. Many pieces use 'you', implicating the reader, and Malone is not afraid to also use the collective 'we', something out of fashion in contemporary poetry, but useful in his exposure of our 'tribal code'. The titular second half, written in single-paragraph prose poems, seems to imply both no easy return to the lyric and a searing imperative to re-think, re-imagine, and re-invent ourselves. There are no easy answers in these poems. They wear a huge range of reference lightly and they beguile with prose sentences that come to seem the very stuff of poetry – a difficult thing to achieve. From MOOCs to the Poundshop, from Churchill's cock-ups to Photoshopping our legacies, Malone takes us on a dizzying ride through both popular and esoteric culture, and yet this work does not disappear into its own scholarship or cynicism, but keeps providing earned, if transitory, glimpses of the human need for meaning: '*Moon, moon!* he says, as if the word holds the heft of all things' ('Commuter'). Somewhat reminiscent of the early work of Geoffrey Hill, perhaps most particularly of *Mercian Hymns*, Malone's work manages to convey the anguish of a deeply moral sensibility by playfully upending and reinventing traditional lyric tropes and by using the prose poem as a form which provides both a scaffold and a restraint for his uncompromising vision. Beware though, he may be addressing you: 'Thank you for your neo-concern'; and 'be advised, your poppy / is not mine' ('Dear Revisionist').

Equally interested in our present predicament is poet Miriam Gamble, whose book *What Planet*, her third collection, is full of brio. She draws us in to a kind of 'Wonderland', lest we develop, as that poem has it, a face 'as blank as a moon'. The voice here is bemused and self-ironizing, 'No one is more confused than me / as to what is meant by it' ('Odradek Returns') – but this is serious play and the poet seems to be asking what we are to make of our lives on the planet right now. Often using 'you' and a sometimes off-stage, sometimes on-stage, speaker as 'I' within the same poem, Gamble plays with perspective, with memory, with time, and with language itself. In this work, the inner map is also that of the lived world, and the latter, she seems to say, is by turns astounding, surreal, demanding, and dark. Gamble uses the line to swerve between knowingness and a kind of implied lament in ways which would not work in the hands of a poet less interested in diction:

> Instead of greenery, you have stripped-
> backery; instead of mammals, the mutant cleg.
>   – 'LEÒDHASACH'

Five untitled sections, the first ending with 'Coda', create the overall effect of overture and four symphonic movements. The poems speak across and back to each other using echoes, syntactical riffs, and re-morphed phrases, all also implying a kind of postmodern – yet still yearning – sensibility which may or may not have any safe place to lodge.

There's a nod to a MacNeicean inheritance, and typically of Gamble's contemporary understanding, this is almost akin to a musical sampling as in 'The Oak That Was Not There': 'The clocks went forward, the clocks went back' and 'the hands of the second went chop, chop, chop'. But there's more to this evocation of MacNeice, as Gamble shares a kind of askance scepticism with her countryman, a metaphysic of the world that finds its true shape in propulsive lyrics and syntactic sparkiness. The obsession with time (also shared with MacNeice) reveals itself later in the book as bound to a deep loss and to what has been 'vacated'. In the end, what appeared to be sheer verve turns out to be hard-won, as the poet trusts her distinctive juxtapositions and swerves to manage language into a repository of emotion. Gamble seems to have a poetic finger on the pulse of how we live now. She is in complete control of her 'gladsome hue of territory' – a fact also noted by the judges of The Pigott Poetry Prize 2020 when awarding Gamble Ireland's richest poetry award for this, her third collection. As judge Ian McMillan says, 'In terrible and turbulent times poetry can offer us a map out of lockdown ... So many Irish poets are working at the height of their powers, wrestling with language to make it fit the world we live in'. It is good to see Gamble's work, already a recipient of a Somerset Maugham Award, recognised in this way.

Gerry Murphy's collection *The Humours of Nothingness* presents short sharp satires as well as narrative memory-based poems, and the book is laced with engaging humour and self-deprecation. Using predominantly short lines, Murphy is not so much interested in how the line operates but rather in pace, in punchiness, and in how best to zoom in on the object of derision or fun. At times, the mordant humour is peppered with a range of reference that keeps it fresh and at other times the laughter turns out to be hollow as the reader is tripped up and incriminated as a culprit. There are some memorable (and some send-up) uses of the haiku form. Here's 'The Thirties' in its entirety:

> Ah, what a decade:
> a scenic railway ending
> in a gas chamber.

There are appearances by Paul Durcan, François Villon, and Stalin; and an encounter with a bewildered Diogenes, 'his fabled lamp finally blown out' ('In Greece'), and Don José 'haunting the Plaza de Toros' ('Seville'). Throughout, there's a distinct presence of the poet himself, self-admonishing but also hopeful; sometimes earnest but mostly tongue in cheek. The two sets of poems which leave their mark on the reader are the vignettes from childhood which bristle with loss and those pieces which, in an almost Brechtian way, address war and yes, the pity of it. 'War & Peace' – which Murphy notes is '*after Yehuda Amichai*'– sets up this sequence, establishing the never-ending cycle from arms-making into violence with a detour into art in between. 'Just Saying' has the whisky-heir, Jameson, in the Congo, buying an eleven-year-old to hand her 'to some cannibals' so he could sketch 'while they butchered her'. It takes some insouciance to place this next to 'Cannibal', where the speaker who has taken 'a sizeable / chunk of flesh' from his brother's shoulder is denied supper by his mother and ends the scene, 'But hey, I had already eaten.' It is a calculated nonchalance however, one designed to poke the reader, and it succeeds but also suggests what this work might well do more of. Reading a book of this facility, and particularly in the moments where the poet-speaker seems to doubt the whole endeavour of poetry, it is tempting to wonder what this talent might produce if it were to take itself unironically seriously for perhaps an extended sequence of poems focused on one of the major themes. In the meantime, *The Humours of Nothingness* has much to offer just as it is.

In her fourth collection, *Girlhood*, Julia Copus writes with a measured cadence, producing elegant stanzas that display their debt to tradition, but which subtly upend the politeness of an agreed-upon aesthetic via the myriad of voices of resistance and counterpoint that pepper this work. Lost figures, people under pressure, and key moments in time seized for re-examination are what animate the first section of the book. While mostly allowing the loping rhythm to carry description as well as move-ment back and forth in time, she also delivers stand-out lines which jump from the page: 'We steady our own like an egg in the dip of a spoon' ('The Grievers').

Copus has a restless imagination and in this book it lands where she can forensically examine some aspect of human foible or transaction, turning a light on it, and making the past live in the present. Her ambition for what the poem as an entity can do is boundless, nothing short of playing out unlived life-paths and embodying moments that live again, only brighter. In 'A Thing Once it has Happened' she has three sections, one called 'During' and two called 'Before'. Copus seems to be implying that it is in poems that true time travel is possible, that multiple universes can be held and will meld in her deft handling. There is humour too, and an ability to vary the line to precisely match the intent of each piece. In 'The Great Unburned', she imagines the speakers, '*the witches you forgot to burn*', speaking to their antagonists: 'The longer we journey, the more your mind chafes'. We, the readers, are addressed, 'How a soul of your sort longs for those dark nights!' It is a poem of two mirroring halves, though with pointed variations. Copus calls this form 'specular' – and the doubling back on itself here works to emphasise the metaphorical reach, commenting on the staid and the stale, everything Copus is clearly not about.

In other poems, Copus deals with apparently ordinary moments, looking back to what may be her father's boyhood, and taking us to gardens and train lines and into telephone conversations. She has the knack of using detail to capture elements of the natural world and moments of personal quest with equal accuracy. We meet her 'goosed and fretful, pootling / among the mirrored pillars and caramel- / coloured wood panelling of Oscar's' ('Sunday Morning at Oscar's'), and we experience her unease in 'Waking late', appreciating 'the fidgety shadows, / the lightly falling blossom'.

The second half of *Girlhood* is an exploration of the sensibility of Marguerite Pantaine, who attempted to murder the actor Huguette Duflos, and it is based on French psychoanalyst Jacques Lacan's meetings with his subject. Lacan's assumptions, his patronising stance, his mistimed interventions, are all imagined with precision. But it is the sections devoted to Marguerite which sizzle. Here, the deadening requirement of the casebook entries are subverted by a voice that is apt in its oddity, compelling in its pursuit of self-knowledge. It is also where Copus experiments most with form. 'Knife' sees Marguerite describe *an interior haunting* where, in longer and then shorter lines, we see her up close with the knife, 'my gloved thumb working / back and forth along its spine'. In these sections, we keep returning to the consulting room in a cycle which seems to reflect the struggle for whose voice will be loudest and last longest. The book finishes with a haunting short lyric, 'Stories', set on a midsummer night. It is classic Copus, bringing time and memory forward like a taste:

> So lies the past,
> no further. You do not need to get up
>
> & stand on tiptoe at the hedge to know
> that what you hear are the people you love.

Gerard Smyth

FACES, FACES

Eavan Boland, *The Historians* (Carcanet Press, 2020), £10.99.

Eavan Boland would surely have been overjoyed by the awarding of this year's Nobel Prize for Literature to Louise Glück, a poet she greatly admired and with whom she had certain things in common: in the work of both poets, emotional truth is expressed in a personal language that has always been clear, precise, and candid.

In Boland's case, those qualities are reflected in her poetry of retrieval and redress, and about that poetry of a lifetime she tells us, in 'The Fire Gilder', the opening poem of *The Historians*:

> My subject is the part wishing plays in
> the way villages are made
> to vanish, in the way I learned
> to separate memory from knowledge ...

That separation of memory from knowledge has been one of the consistencies in her work. In the title poem of this posthumously-published collection, she tells us that 'Those who wrote that story / laboured to own it', but the poet herself has a different perspective, defiantly rejecting the received and handed-down version of history and the past, which she regarded as one of exclusion, a history damaged by its gaps and absences, its fractures and fissures. Instead, she arrived at a different realisation:

> Say the word *history*: I see
> your mother, mine.

These are women with inescapable tasks: 'To stop memory becoming history. / To stop words healing what should not be healed.' Throughout her work, Boland has used words to interrogate, understand, and re-define the legacy of the past. In another poem, she addresses a poet who 'died young', saying: 'Your words disturbed my earth. They changed my mind', but she also acknowledges that her own words 'offer little comfort and less peace' ('For a Poet Who Died Young').

In 'Silenced' (from *Domestic Violence*, 2007), she writes of the Greek mythological figure Philomel, after rape by her brother-in-law and having her tongue cut out, being 'determined to tell her story / another way'. That was essentially Boland's mission from the beginning: the telling of stories another way. It was a mission that shaped her work to the very last, as these fine valedictory poems demonstrate.

One poem in particular, 'Eviction' (section VII of the title sequence), reminds us that she was a poet who set out to find and put on record the 'story that needed to be told' ('The Historians') – this she has previously achieved in such powerful poems as 'Quarantine' and 'Making Money'. 'Eviction' is prompted by an incident directly out of her own family annals and begins:

> Back from Dublin, my grandmother
> finds an eviction notice on her door.

It is not only the incident itself, the fact of this woman facing the loss of her home, that engages and enrages the poet, but also the manner of how it was reported in the *Drogheda Argus and Leinster Journal* in 1904 (as the poem notes), as a kind of footnote to the larger dramas:

> A woman leaves a courtroom in tears.
> A nation is rising to the light.
> History notes the second not the first.

The invisibility of women in Irish society is also the subject of another superbly concise poem, 'Anonymous', in which Boland thinks about the part played in the drama of history by another 'near relative', who 'carried messages, / communications, worn- / out documents, / ferrying revolt / to the far corners / of Haddington Road /and O'Connell Street.' The poem ends on one of those declaratory notes that she often employs as a punch-line to a meditation: 'That / is history. This / is only poetry.'

In a sense, *The Historians* presents us – due to the sudden circumstance of her death – with not only her concluding poems, but poems which are a final and fitting reiteration and summation of the sustained narrative of Boland's quest to strike out on behalf of those left in the margins, or 'outside history'. In several of these, she revisits familiar and abiding themes from throughout the course of her career, creating a loop with a return to the scenes and settings of earlier poems: the suburban garden that looks to the Dublin hills; the city and its river which have always been central to her work; memories of her artist mother – the impulse behind some of her most memorable poems, recurring again in the haunting expression of love that is 'Translating the Word *Home*', in which we encounter the artist/mother 'painting a Connemara summer'. The 'infant daughters' of her much-loved poems of motherhood appear again too, this time as the mothers of her grandchildren in 'Without End', reminding us that life itself is 'the one storyteller / with the one story / that had no ending'.

And once more in these pages we accompany Boland among the city monuments that represent to her the old Ireland about which she asks, in the poem 'Broken': *'how could I ever have loved you / if I never believed you?'*

> To right and left of me old patriots,
> their mouths stuffed with bronze,
> their words falling onto winter plinths.

Her affection for inherited and found things has been a common thread, and here resurfaces in the poem 'The Barograph' ('I found it on the quays, / a rectangle of wood, / a barograph, its pen arm inking paper'). 'The Lamplighter', a poem that continues her preoccupation with the shadow-world of the past and one of the most moving and striking in the book, locates us in her city of ghosts: Dublin. The bygone lamplighter of the poem is also,

> a small
> lawmaker re-drawing street
> corners and neighbourhoods
> in our city

In general, Boland's language moves at a measured pace, her lines making a slow advance to arrive at their revelatory moment. After her apprentice books – and particularly from *Night Feed* on – she settled into the plain-spoken idiom and tone that has so fruitfully served and accommodated her purpose and convictions. However, the lyric elegance of her language in no way dilutes her critical perspective, or the disciplined rage that inter-sects with serene acts of remembrance.

Boland has always had a wonderful capacity to isolate and evoke the mood and detail of particular moments, doing so with almost understated description and intimacy, and in several poems here we see it at work: 'Rain', 'How We Were Transfigured' (with its dusky intro, 'Now when darkness starts / in mid-afternoon, / when evening shows an unwelcome / half-sliced winter moon'), and the elegiac 'This Garden', which begins:

> Awake late at night what I see is
> faces, faces, their radiance. And realize
> I will never see them again.

These are crisp and beautiful poems for a career to end on, a career that has also been responsible for a widening of the community of women poets and of poetry's readers. Writing about the work of another poet she admired, Adrienne Rich, she once made two particular points: that it contested 'the structure of the poetic tradition', and was 'rooted deep in a human life'. Both of these observations are equally true of the work of

Eavan Boland, who tenaciously and uncompromisingly remained a poet who, like those suffragettes commemorated in the book's final poem, 'had the faith / That voices can be raised. / Can be heard.'

Ailbhe Darcy

RECENT DOCUMENTARY POETRY IN PERFORMANCE

Kimberly Campanello's three-hour-long performance of her work
MOTHERBABYHOME (2019), recorded at UCD library for the Irish
Poetry Reading Archive, is not a dance but a poetry reading. Still, I think
of dance when I watch it. Perhaps Campanello has purposely courted
this echo of another art form: her feet are bare, her hair is up, and she
is clad in a black outfit reminiscent of a leotard. There is no podium or
microphone. As the performance unfolds, she moves around the space
freely – as poets giving readings conventionally do not – sometimes
sitting cross-legged or crouching or even getting down on hands and
knees. Pages are strewn on the carpet about her, so that when she moves,
she has to be careful not to step on them. Sometimes she pauses to tidy
them up, stacking them into loose heaps to make space for her body.
MOTHERBABYHOME takes the form of a whopping sheaf of loose-leaf
vellum pages in an oak box, so reading it requires certain physical
gestures distinct from the reading of a book. In performance, Campanello
carries out these gestures on our behalf. She lifts the heavy lid from the
box and places it carefully down on the ground; she leans in and pulls
pages out of the shadows, delving deeper, with greater effort, as the box
grows emptier. She holds the translucent vellum pages close and squints
to make out the words, which are sometimes blurred or fragmented,
obscured by other words or printed very small or faintly. Only six copies
of *MOTHERBABYHOME* were made, originally, and five of these are
housed in libraries. The space in which Campanello moves for this
performance, carpeted and lined with books, is the same space in which
the reader is likely to encounter the box and, in order to read the poem,
the reader will have to make at least some of the same gestures. It is as
if Campanello is showing us how this dance, or ritual, is meant to be
performed by us.

In his book *Distant Reading: Performance, Readership, and Consumption
in Contemporary Poetry* (2005), Peter Middleton muses on how an audience
might respond to the performance of a dance. One response is to inter-
pret the dance as symbolic: an audience might decide that the performing
bodies and their gestures stand for something in the real world. *That
ballerina is a fawn; those caressing gestures mean love.* Another response is
aesthetic: an audience might find the form of the dance beautiful. A third
response is intertextual: they might see in this dance echoes of other
dances. But there is another response, Middleton suggests, that is
'kinesthetic … cognitive, but not linguistic, in which the audience senses
the movements of the dancers in terms of their own bodies'. The body

in the audience imagines itself making the gestures it sees being made on the stage, with 'no necessary intervening stage of conscious interpretation between seeing the dancer and this inward imaginative movement'. It is this aspect of dance, I imagine, which is most difficult for the critic to capture and convey; and it is this response that I notice in myself as I watch Campanello's performance. What are these inward imaginative gestures that I am making? And to what end?

MOTHERBABYHOME is not so much about Tuam Mother and Baby Home as it is about the public conversation around that subject. To stretch the dance metaphor, while some of the words in this poem come from the weighty testimonies of survivors, relatives, and witnesses, the wider public discourse is shown to be a set of grotesquely empty verbal gestures, a polka in which multiple dancers skip free of any blame, responsibility, or concrete action. At one point, Campanello repeats and remixes the words of Father Pádraig McCarthy, who wrote in the Catholic journal *The Furrow* that 'burial in an unmarked grave does not necessarily mean "disrespect" to the dead. Usually it means the people concerned had other priorities on their minds at the time.' Campanello's poem is, as its headnote declares, 'composed entirely of text taken from historical archives and contemporary media and other sources related to the Home', including files provided to the author by the historian Catherine Corless. I get the impression that the 'sources related to the Home' include emails or letters that were addressed to Campanello *about* the poem itself as it was being written, so that the text is weirdly self-reflexive, commenting on its own intervention in the public discourse. It is part of a tiny explosion of documentary works in Irish poetry, which also includes Christodoulos Makris's *this is no longer entertainment: A Documentary Poem* (2019), Rachael Hegarty's *May Day 1974* (2019) and Cherry Smyth's *Famished* (2019). Following in the American tradition of documentary poetry, for which the mother text is Muriel Rukeyser's *Book of the Dead* (1938), all of these new works bear witness to dark, dark episodes in Irish social history.

I find it interesting that two of these works of documentary poetry – Campanello's and Smyth's – exist not only as texts, but as virtuoso performances. On its face, the documentary poem, a mish-mash of texts that don't belong to the poet's voice, and often spliced together in a somewhat deadpan, faux-objective manner, is an odd sort of poem to want to perform. But the performances of *MOTHERBABYHOME* and *Famished* are startling and intriguing, even disturbing and powerful. I suspect that they have insights to offer us about the cultural work poetry can do and about the strategies available to us when we harness the body or the voice in poetry's service. (Full disclosure: I met Campanello when we were both invited to read our poetry at Prague Microfestival in 2018, and we have kept in touch since.)

In an essay on 'The Lost Children of Tuam' in *The New York Times* in 2017, Dan Barry wrote:

> Even today, the Irish say they do death well. Local radio newscasts routinely end with a recitation of death notices. In a country where the culture of Catholicism, if not its practice, still holds sway, this alerts the community to a familiar ritual: the wake at the home, the funeral Mass, the long gathering at the pub, the memorial Mass a month later, and the anniversary Mass every year thereafter.
> [...]
> Respect for burial grounds runs deep, with crowds gathering in their local cemetery once a year to pray as a priest blesses the dead within. This reverence for the grave may derive from centuries of land dispossession, or passed-on memories of famine corpses in the fields and byways, or simply be linked to a basic desire expressed by the planting of a headstone: To be remembered.

Barry's observation that we Irish take pride in our funerals and commemorations – indeed, that we see our rituals around death as integral to our very identity – takes on a terrible irony in the face of what happened to the children who died at Tuam Mother and Baby Home. A little over halfway through *MOTHERBABYHOME*, Campanello reprints Barry's assertion, 'Even today, the Irish say they do death well', repeating each word twice, requiring us to spend a little longer with the idea than we might have done in reading Barry's essay. The visual effect created on the page is of blurring – as if we are seeing double. This is in a 796-page text in which every single page bears the name of a baby or child whose death was patently not 'done well'. The particular page on which Barry's quote appears bears the name of Bridget Murphy, who, we learn, died in 1944 at the age of two and a quarter months; in performance, Bridget Murphy's name must be read aloud immediately before Barry's remark. In the absence of adequate rituals by which we might honour Bridget Murphy and face up to what happened to her, I wonder if Campanello is offering us another kind of ritual in the shape of her poem and its performance.

The idea that poetry is, or can be, a form of ritual is perhaps a tired one. It risks such an abstraction of the words 'poetry' and 'ritual' that we are left with nothing specific enough to be useful. All the same, it is tempting to think of the performances of recent Irish documentary poems in terms of Jack Santino's notions of the 'ritualesque' and the 'performative commemoration'. Santino, who works on performance studies and folklore, uses these words to discuss how phenomena as various as Bloody Sunday commemorations, Gay Pride parades, Orange Order marches, and American anti-drunk driving programmes involve an attempt to transform their participants through their ritualised participation:

> When citizens of Derry City hold their Bloody Sunday commemoration event, images of those slain on that occasion are displayed and paraded. This is an act of commemoration and mourning, but the entire event can also be seen as an attempt to see to it that justice is done; to influence the minds and hearts of onlookers, spectators and participants.
>
> — 'PERFORMING IRELAND'

Santino coins the word 'ritualesque' to describe how such an event might ask participants, as in a religious ritual, to gather around highly-charged images and go through a set of symbolic actions, but with the purpose of social communion and transformation rather than sacramental transformation and communion with one's god. Perhaps a poem can, in comparable ways, be 'ritualesque' – an act of commemoration that requires us to spend prolonged time with a subject, as a way of honouring that subject, but also as a way of affecting what we think and do in the world.

One characteristic of the documentary poem is that, although it is a carefully-curated act of rhetoric on the part of an author, it tends to mimic an archive, presenting itself as a collection of pieces of documentary 'evidence', which readers themselves must actively piece together. (I do not mean here to ignore the fact that historical archives themselves are always curated and may have rhetorical designs on the user, but I am trying to articulate one way in which the experience of reading a documentary poem differs from reading a poem that presents itself as an original expression in a novel combination of words, spoken by a lyric 'I'.) The reader is asked, by MOTHERBABYHOME, to reach into an archive and piece together the documents found within. In other words, the reader must perform the role of a historian or investigator – specifically, in this case, a member of the Mother and Baby Homes Commission of Investigation – but in a ritualised, pre-determined way. The purpose may be to commemorate the dead, but it is also to transform the reader's relationship with the events and materials surrounding their death.

Middleton suggests that, generally, at a conventional poetry reading, when the poet is reading aloud a set of lyric poems, the poet 'performs authorship, becoming in the process a divided subject by reproducing language constructed into a poem at some time prior to the reading, while reading aloud as if it were a spontaneous speech act arising in the present.' The words uttered are temporarily given a body as their context, 'as if the reader were showing what it means for a life to say these words, because the physical presence of the speaker acts as their warrant for their relevance to a specific body, point of view, and history.' In other words, when we stand at a microphone or podium and read aloud our poems, we are performing ourselves in the act of composing those words. Campanello's performance of *MOTHERBABYHOME* does something different, I think. Instead of performing an idealised moment of writing – performing the self from whom the poem issues forth – Campanello performs an idealised moment of reading; and by doing so, she steps into the role of the community who must engage in the poem's 'performative commemoration' and thereby be transformed.

On the fourth page of Campanello's text (dedicated to Mary Kelly, who died aged six months), the text reads: 'The practice was to offer no pain relief as suffering was regarded as part of her punishment.' The line comes from an article in *The Irish Times* by Lorna Siggins in 2014, reporting testimony from a mother who gave birth in a Mother and Baby Home on the Navan Road. As a piece of journalism, Siggins's story already bears witness to cruelty at Mother and Baby Homes, offering emotionally affecting first-person testimony, and already exists in the public sphere; in other words, it already does work that a politically-engaged lyric poem might hope to do. Campanello's poem does almost the opposite: it 'buries' the testimony in a box and removes it from the first-person narrative that gives it rhetorical and emotional authority. It removes the words' referents, so that we are forced to imagine for ourselves (though heaven knows we can well imagine) who '*she*' might be, and why she might be punished. And it makes the text itself harder to read, using idiosyncratic punctuation, spacing on the page and italicisation to add what Cole Swensen calls 'noise'. 'Noise', Swensen writes, is understood in information theory as 'any signal, interruption or disturbance in the channel of communication that alters the quantity or quality of transmitted information', but in poetry is better understood as 'often intentional and aimed at preventing the suppression of imagination that complete certainty can cause.' Many of Campanello's strategies in *MOTHERBABYHOME* seem devised to 'prevent the suppression of imagination' that is caused by our thinking that we already know, all too well, the story of Tuam Mother and Baby Home. Perhaps our transformation is meant to be from passive witnesses to active seekers of justice. What the oak box requires of us is to make a set of physical gestures that mimic digging into the archives or – more horrifyingly yet – reaching into a mass grave and uncovering buried children.

Although *MOTHERBABYHOME* obviously takes the American tradition of documentary poetry for its primary influence, Campanello has mentioned that Thomas Kinsella's poem *Butcher's Dozen* (1972) was also an important precursor for her. Like Campanello's poem, *Butcher's*

Dozen is more concerned with the public inquiry into the event than with the event itself. The form of Kinsella's poem mimics, to some extent, the form of the Widgery Report, visiting the Bogside area of Derry where the 'Bloody Sunday' massacre took place and describing the landscape, then recounting a series of eyewitness accounts. While Widgery interviewed the survivors and perpetrators, Kinsella 'interviews' the dead. Similarly, Campanello's poem takes the form of the inquiry it condemns – a text that is made up of large swathes of silent white space, it seems to accuse the Mother and Baby Homes Commission of being less a form of justice than a means of delay. Originally scheduled to issue its final report by February 2018, the Commission has been granted several extensions and has still not published a final report. The sheer size of Campanello's poem allows for patterns and repetitions to artfully accumulate; at times, in performance, Campanello garbles or stutters over the repetition, and the most repetitive sections of all – as when she reads aloud a long list of causes of death – put me in mind of Laurie Anderson's use of repetition to render language automatic and dehumanised. While Kinsella's *Butcher's Dozen* imaginatively allows ghosts to speak, the dead at Tuam Mother and Baby Home are disturbingly silent in Campanello's text; their names, ages, and the dates of their deaths are all we have of them. At the end of Campanello's performance, she places the last page on the library floor and walks away. I found myself wanting her to stay and pick the pages back up off the floor, to return them to their box. The box is at once ironic and sincere: at once a knowing, glamorised fantasy of an archive, and a coffin, it speaks to the dignity these children weren't granted in death, but it grants them something, too – it is, in itself, a dignifying act. That is, the box of *MOTHERBABYHOME* is a kind of monument, but the kind of monument that Emily Mark-FitzGerald has in mind in her essay 'Commemoration and the Performance of Irish Famine Memory' when she points out that monuments are both the product and the site of repeated performances of remembering – they can only *remain* monuments as long as they are sites where active remembering repeatedly takes place.

Famished (2019), Cherry Smyth's work of documentary poetry about the Irish famine, seems determined to work against the active forgetting that can be the other, more problematic side of the monument – as when Famine memorials reduce events in nineteenth-century Ireland to a set of images full of emotional pull but devoid of any specific historical context. A mix of archival matter and lyric poetry that, by its very substantiality, heralds many hours spent attending to the history of the famine years, *Famished* counters the notion that 'much of the material evidence of the Famine was erased', as perhaps some of us (in this quote, given voice by Marian Eide in 'Famine Memory and Contemporary Irish Poetry') are inclined to imagine. The book is dedicated to named young women, whose fates, after their forced emigration, are known – Eliza Taafe, an eighteen-year-old Dubliner who was declared insane and institution-alised upon arrival in Adelaide; and Alice Ball, a sixteen-year-old from Enniskillen, who was made pregnant by her Melbourne employer and drowned herself in the Yarra river. Towards the end of the book, Taafe and Ball are given voice in poems of their own. Throughout *Famished*, the judgments of the history books are quoted without commentary, as they segue from outright condemnation to a tacit forgiveness of England's role in the catastrophe. *Famished* itself is unabashedly accusa-tory; the word 'England' or 'English' crops up again and again. The final few pages of *Famished* make clear the links to our own complicity in poverty and suffering in the present day, culminating in an ambivalent reflection on art's role in making suffering palatable – in memorialising that which should be scrutinised and understood.

In interview, Smyth stresses her poetry's international influences, but her commitment to narrative in *Famished* suggests that one precursor for her poem is John Montague's *The Rough Field* (1972), a text which similarly opens out from the self to an engagement with the social history in which that self is located, via a sequence of lyric poems cut with quotes from other texts. Smyth, like Montague, never moves far from lyric and from the various techniques we bundle under the idea of poetic 'craft', though at times she pointedly denies these techniques their full power, especially where they risk a sense of conclusion or complacency. While some sections of *Famished* are free verse, and bring spaces and gaps into the line of the poem, spreading out to use the full field of the page, at other moments Smyth deploys variations on the sonnet form. 'English Recipes', for instance, is a fifteen-line sonnet: once achieved, conclusively, it suddenly opens out again with the interjection, *"And why don't they eat fish?"*

Despite its loyalty to narrative lyric, *Famished* often refuses its own musicality, as if sensible of the comfort music can be. The nursery rhyme chant 'One potato, two potato, three potato, four' provides a refrain for the sequence in its opening pages, but instead of gathering steam, gradually shrinks away. 'The Coffin-Land, Ballyliffin' begins with long lines and a swinging rhythm:

> The bell unrung, the song unsung,
> the wind their only keening.
> No ritual fastened them to the land.
> No wake to give an easing.

This song-like metre is swiftly dropped and the poem concludes with short, cut-up lines delivered in the same deadpan way as much of the rest of the text:

> His grave, a dent
> in earth,
> five stones
> on five parts of him.

The white of the page that would ordinarily follow a lyric poem like this – signalling the time the reader is expected to spend absorbing and pondering the poem – is disrupted by a footnoted quote from another source, denying us a moment of closure and contemplation.

In the lines quoted above – 'No wake to give an easing' – and elsewhere in the text, *Famished* explicitly craves a ritual to acknowledge the famine dead, but also implies the impossibility of ever staging an adequate one. The short poem 'A Mass' is a fantasy of what an adequate ritual might look like:

> In my Famine mass, 2 million people
> line the east coast, standing, seaward;
> 1.5 million line the west, lying down
> along the Wild Atlantic Way. It's filmed
> by a drone. A remembrance mass.
> A mass whisper.

Elsewhere, the text declares:

> There is an energy
> required for loss,
> for singing loss,
> for losing,
> that too much grief
> does utterly consume.

These reflections become self-reflexive when the text of *Famished* becomes a performance, as it did, for instance, in Cardiff this February. (I invited Smyth to perform *Famished* at Seren Poetry Festival in my role as a lecturer at Cardiff University.) Smyth, who grew up in Portstewart but has lived in London for many years, has a clipped, brisk voice capable of business-like matter-of-factness but also of searing contempt. She reads us the facts of the famine: the Lumper potato, the absentee landlord, the suffrage limited to property owners, the twenty shovels shared between 4,000 people, the 1.5 million dead at home, the dead at sea 'too many to know'. Her voice is icy, her expression steely, as she reads aloud Thomas Carlyle's declaration that, 'Ireland is like a half-starved rat that crosses the path of an elephant.' She reads aloud snatches of nursery rhyme in a sing-song voice that might test an audience's patience. She coldly reports comments made to her as a young woman, newly-arrived in London in the 1980s: 'maybe the stereotype of the Irish being thick is because you only had potatoes to eat and the diet affected your intelligence'.

What makes Smyth's performance of *Famished* extraordinary – and 'ritualesque' – is her decision to collaborate with Lauren Kinsella, an experimental vocalist, in performing it. After a couple of minutes of Smyth's reading, Kinsella begins to sing alongside or against Smyth, snatches of song that take off from the text – *one potato, two potato; haul in the bowlin', Kitty was my darlin'* – but also, gradually, improvised sounds, noises, wailing, guttural growls and barks that sometimes drown out the text or compete with it. Kinsella has a gorgeous, ethereal singing voice that she uses, in this performance, for grimy, down-in-the-dirt, animalistic yawls as much as for lilting and lullabying. Sometimes she whispers. Sometimes, for several minutes at a time, she stops singing at all and we shift uncomfortably in her silence, wondering what's coming for us next. Kinsella's crooning and caterwauling are firmly in the tradition of Sinéad O'Connor's (and Dolores O'Riordan's) 'exploration of trauma through the medium of the human voice', as described by Emer Nolan, and which in turn draws on folk song, particularly the lament or 'keen'. This is an artistic mode that has been central to women's poetic production in Ireland since medieval times, and one which has often been a space for political outspokenness, even a radical space for speaking truth to power. Nolan writes of O'Connor, though she might as easily be writing about Kinsella in this context:

> The modulations of her voice between purity and anger do not con-
> form to any predictable pattern. Its 'stridency' is never far removed
> from its lyric or spiritual qualities. Even in its soaring mode, the voice
> has a 'catch' or flaw in its purity which comes not from any sense
> of muscular effort or strain, but from a refusal of the emancipatory
> seductions that a clearly struck high note, with its shine and finish,
> seems to offer.
>
> – 'SINÉAD O'CONNOR: THE STORY OF A VOICE'

It is hard to tell how everyone in the audience responds to this peculiar, disorienting performance. They came, presumably, expecting a conventional poetry reading. Some are clearly enthralled and deeply moved; there are tears at question time. Some are stony-faced. Some look uncomfortable. Some are surely embarrassed. Just as the keen, in traditional funeral rituals, offers a hyperbolic performance of the mourners' own grief, Kinsella is singing on *our* behalf – her mutters, soars and wails voice *our* lament. Our discomfort with the performance is a discomfort with the identity we claim: our national identity – since the room in which I saw *Famished* performed had many Irish emigrants and members of the diaspora in it, alongside British audience members – but also our identity as empathetic poetry-readers. We are prepared to be moved by a poem, even to quiet tears – but *this?*

In its text form, there is no doubt that Smyth's arrangement of historical evidence has a rhetorical force: *Famished* is an argumentative text, in the best sense. It answers to Kenneth Burke's description of rhetorical poetry as 'the use of words by human agents to form attitudes or to induce actions in other agents', even if 'the kinds of assent evoked have no overt, practical outcome'. The poem changes entirely in performance, however. Part of the work Kinsella does in the performance of *Famished* is the addition of 'noise' in Swensen's sense. If in literature, as Swensen says, noise is 'aimed at preventing the suppression of imagination that complete certainty can cause', Kinsella's noise breaks open a space, around a text which has a great deal of rhetorical certainty and pre-determined meaning, for the imagination. The uncertainty that emerges is far more unsettling and challenging than Burke's rhetorical 'assent'.

Richard Hayes

OUTSIDE THE SACRED HOUSE

Dairena Ní Chinnéide, *deleted* (Salmon Poetry, 2019), €12.
Catherine Barry, *A Beautiful Pain* (Salmon Poetry, 2020), €12.
Ross Thompson, *Threading the Light* (Dedalus Press, 2019), €12.50.
Polina Cosgrave, *My Name Is* (Dedalus Press, 2020), €12.50.
Chris Murray, *Gold Friend* (Turas Press, 2020), €12.
Leeanne Quinn, *Some Lives* (Dedalus Press, 2020), €12.50.

For much of the twentieth century, Irish poetry grappled, intellectually and emotionally, with the tensions described in the famous encounter between Stephen Dedalus and his Dean of Studies, an Englishman, in *A Portrait of the Artist as a Young Man*. 'He felt with a smart of dejection that the man to whom he was speaking was a countryman of Ben Jonson', writes Joyce, with a dismayed Stephen reflecting, 'The language in which we are speaking is his before it is mine.' Serious Irish poets of the last hundred years and more have engaged, with varying degrees of enthusiasm and explicitness, in a negotiation with the English language and the English poetic tradition, the search being for a set of rhetorical approaches to match Irish experience, for a language and, as Heaney has it, for 'symbols adequate to our predicament'.

Of course, at the heart of this is the (post-) colonial experience of dispossession, so frequently Irish poetry has a particular engagement with landscape and territory: Kavanagh's much quoted 'Epic' legitimises the land of Ireland or (again to refer to Heaney) 'gives the place credit for existing, assists at its real topographical presence, dwells upon it and accepts it as the definitive locus of the given world.' For similar reasons, the post-Romantic personal lyric occupies the central position in terms of poetic mode, granting, as it were, the (post-colonial) subject also a hitherto unrecognised validity. Most often secular, these engagements and negotiations nonetheless are uncomfortable with Modernist profanity and both make reference to the metaphysical frameworks inherited from Yeats and the Celtic Twilight – sentimental ideas of some elemental source for Irish identity, most often the land – and at the same time take account of the distortions that have come about by virtue of Irish sectarianism and the theocracy that existed south of the border until the 1990s. These concerns are significant; the stakes, to put it another way, are high through twentieth-century Irish poetry, for there is a political, even a moral dimension to these intellectual concerns insofar as the imagination – with poetry as its most potent expression – had a role to play in fashioning the Ireland that took shape in the period between the birth of

Yeats and, say, the death of Heaney. Amongst the major voices, discomfort with that emerging Ireland seems to me to be the abiding note; one cannot read our most celebrated poets since Yeats – Clarke, Kavanagh in the first generation; Mahon, Heaney, Boland, amongst others secondly – without acknowledging their restlessness. 'My soul frets in the shadow of his language', says Stephen Dedalus, after all.

But what are the preoccupations a hundred years on from Joyce? And, especially, do we detect that same note of disquiet in new poetry? Have intellectual concerns shifted in the light of the collapse of the Catholic Church's hegemony in the South, the re-setting of Ireland-UK political relations and a reorientation of Irish politics towards Europe, and globalisation and the increasing diversity of the Irish population, so that Irish-English is now inflected with and heard alongside a wide variety of other European and non-European languages and traditions? What are the intellectual interests of the new Ireland and how are these reflected in the style and subject matter of new Irish poetry? The six collections considered here are a reasonable sample with which to open out some of these questions.

The collections that most obviously adopt and engage with the tropes and concerns sketched out above are *deleted* by Dairena Ní Chinnéide, *A Beautiful Pain* by Catherine Barry, and Ross Thompson's *Threading the Light*. The conviction with which these poets handle both their material and their method suggests many of the tensions pointed to by Joyce have, in their cases at least, been somewhat resolved. Ní Chinnéide opens her rather gentle, quite beautiful collection with 'Unplugged on the Great Blasket', a poem that obviously pays homage to and connects the poetry with the past: 'We are but flotsam / in the ancient folklore / of this island's people', she writes; 'we tread with care / we give thanks for it.' This note is picked up a number of times elsewhere. The work here is accomplished, the voice confident: 'I loved like a mother,' we read in 'Motherload':

> I wrote like a dervish
> I worshipped my muse
> I did it cause I wanted to.

Catherine Barry's *A Beautiful Pain* also honours both the present and the past. There is, as Barry says in an excellent long poem, 'Going Back to Self', the keynote I think of the book, 'the absolute thrill / of going back to self', and this great celebration of sheer existence runs through the work. 'As you walk the talk,' the collection's final poem, 'Surrender', has it, 'a new you / is fermenting. / You are an embryo of hope. / You already are.' The universe within which this 'you' is inscribed is firmly an

Irish one; the book draws on distinctively Irish phrases and phrasings ('I could mill it down to the 17A', for instance) and is attuned, rhythmically, to oral poetry and the full flavours of Irish speech. There is no lack of ambition in Barry's work – she includes in the collection a number of fine longer poems – and the book is full of energy and interest.

Thompson's excellent *Threading the Light*, the best of these three books, draws on his own life and experience with some powerful poems about family, including the long, brilliant 'Grief is Great'. His frame of reference is expansive, most evident in the second section of the book, 'The New World', where he makes reference to American sources and inspirations and taps into cinematic approaches and traditions. The loose-limbed lyrical approach evident in Ní Chinnéide and Barry is eschewed in favour of a more formal approach; he trusts that an investment in rhyme, rhythm, and shape will hold good, and it invariably does. There are some excellent individual poems here, including 'On Castlerock Beach':

> I beat a frenzied drum to the Bar Mouth
> to retrieve the tiny pink shoe that dropped
>
> from my pocket in all the commotion.
> There, barely within reach on the swelling
> beach, it was, helpless, taunted by the ocean.
> For a moment it was almost claimed but
>
> I picked it up and closed the gap between
> what is God's and what is mine. Close behind
> the water rushed in and out of the void,
> as if to say, "Next time … next time … next time."

In none of these three cases, I submit, is there anxiety and uncertainty evident; this is a poetry that is sure of itself and its world. There is here, in this sense, a resolution to the 'unrest of spirit' of which Joyce writes.

In contrast, the collections by Polina Cosgrave, Chris Murray, and Leeanne Quinn proceed through uncertainty, anxiety, and unease. I think they are the more interesting for it. Cosgrave's *My Name Is*, as is obvious from the book's title, takes the 'problem' of identity as her starting point; 'Don't let go', she urges herself in the final poem in the collection ('Invisible Thread'), because her security within a certain identity is fragile. The act of naming – or unnaming, as it is explored in a curious, dark poem, 'He who unnamed me' – is an act of great power; the self exists, Cosgrave seems to say, and accepts, once it can name and be named. A member of the 'new Irish' as an emigrant from Volgograd, Russia, Cosgrave meditates on the notion of 'home' throughout the collection, insofar as home can be established through that act of naming. In 'Surnames', she writes:

> I'm a Russian girl with an Irish surname,
> who was a Russian girl with a Jewish surname,
> who was a Russian girl with a Russian surname
> who once spent nine months in a belly of
> an Armenian girl with a Russian surname.

Here, the Russian doll offers a marvellous metaphor through which to consider identity questions. 'I am so full of names', she writes in the title poem, not a single one of which (as rehearsed in that poem) is Irish.

If Cosgrave cannot resolve the questions that arise for writers of the 'new' Ireland through the enunciation of a definitive 'name', Chris Murray challenges the possibility of resolution through poetic form. In *Gold Friend*, Murray bends and stretches form, deploying variations in typography, for instance, to startling effect. 'Eve Labouring for 37 hours; the *Yes* poem' opens:

> Great
>   monumental
> Eve in pain.
>
> will bring
> forth a Cain /
>   Abel
> Cannibal.
>
> exhausted stretch
> rather/rather/rather
> rather/rather/rather
> dilate/than die/Yes.

The poems are mesmerising – I think particularly of 'Lament for a lost child' – and very much challenge our sense of what makes for an 'Irish' poem. The unrest visible here is the anxiety associated less with a poetic voice and more with the nature of the poem, requiring the invention and reinvention of poetic devices to convey experience. One is reminded occasionally of Thomas Kinsella's later work.

Finally, we have Leeanne Quinn's *Some Lives*, the most formally accomplished of the books considered here. The poems are mysterious and evasive. She refers to a range of Russian writers – Akhmatova, Mandelstam, Tsvetaeva – and in this way, I think, attunes her imaginative constructs morally and politically. 'This all happened in the distant past', she writes, 'when, in my borrowed coat, / I buried a book.' She – herself? Nadezhda Mandelstam? both? – recalls a man threatening to throw a live mouse onto a hot pan. 'And that could probably / / sum it up,' she says.

> But as the snow sticks
> to the cuff of my coat, I glimpse
> from the corner of my eye the shade
>
> of a future where, warmed
> and absolved, we'll spend our time
> living this down.
>   – 'THE DISTANT PAST'

This is some distance, I think, from the celebratory 'we give thanks for it' of Ní Chinnéide's work, tonally and otherwise. The title poem of the book is a spectacular performance built around an incantation, 'I read a poem about the end of the world.' *Some Lives* is rich and disconcerting. There is nothing peculiarly or obviously 'Irish' about it.

Ní Chinnéide, Barry, and Thompson have produced excellent collections of resonant, sometimes very moving lyric poetry. They write about the known world with fluency and authority, and are utterly convincing in their approach. Cosgrave, Murray and, especially, Quinn write a poetry that is much more unsettling, much less certain, and, if one may put it like this, a poetry with its mind much less made up about what the world is and can be. If the first three collections suggest the resolution of the moral and political questions that arose with the early years of the Irish State, the latter suggest new questions and tensions have emerged. There remains a role, in other words, for poetry in forging the new Ireland. The poet, Yeats rather romantically proclaimed, 'may not stand within the sacred house but lives amid the whirlwinds that beset its threshold.' The contrariness – formally, linguistically, thematically – of some of the work here makes that evident and is to be celebrated.

Ailbhe Ní Ghearbhuigh

TÁ AIBHLÉIS SAN UILE NÍ

> *alles leben besteht*
> *aus elektrizität*
> — Jan Wagner

i
an stoc sin thall
an tamhan fliuch
seoltar sruthanna
trína chroí bog

ii
fiú an laghairt bhándearg
a théaltaíonn isteach
sa seomra folctha
is tú ar saoire
sna críocha teo;
tá faghairt le feiscint
ina shúil gheiceo

iii
trá shóibhéadach an Domhnaigh
slabanna coincréite ina mbacainn
foirgneamh díthógtha ar an aill
sreanga dubha beo ina bhfeamainn

iv
lá na seacht síon
cuislíonn sí tríom.

Ailbhe Ní Ghearbhuigh

DORDÁN AIBHLÉISE OS MO CHIONN

éiríonn ina challán
méadaíonn
tonnaíonn
an spéir ina tollán
cúngaíonn
fadaíonn os mo chomhair,
mé ag teitheadh, ag éalú
ó shaighneáin ghéarsholais
a dhallann
a threascraíonn,
an chré á bánú fúm.
Bronnann tú orm súile nua,
buí is lonrach, súile cait,
sciath in aghaidh an doininn
a lasann tríd an doircheacht
a bhaineann preab as neacha
idir bheoibh is mhairbh.

Ailbhe Ní Ghearbhuigh

DORDÁN FOICHE IM BHÉAL

Airím a sciatháin ag greadadh:
Fágtar gág dóite ar an dteanga
Is blas loiscthe ar an gcarball.

Rian ceilge ar bharr mo chinn,
Rabharta fola ag brúchtaíl aníos,
Binn an phian ag broidearnach.

Diarmuid Johnson

AN UBH FUISEOIGE

Tá galar an tsiúil ar chlanna an duine
Ionainn feasta níl oiriseamh ná cónaí.

Adhraimid déithe buí na hiasachta
Paidir an chóngair: is é a bhíonn ar ár mbéal.

Sinne feasta is dall ar gach sean-mhall-iontas
Sinne is dall fós ar shean-sean-mhall-áilleacht an tsaoil.

Ach ubh fuiseoige: sin é a fuaireas ar na dumhcha!
Bhí braon de dhrúcht na maidine ag glinniúint uirthi fós.

Gur chuireas an bhlaosc mhín sin le toll mo chluaise
Seanmheandar síoraí dom ag éisteacht:

Bhí dóthain ceoil i gcroí na huibhe bige
Le stad a bhaint as mire mhór na linne.

Doireann Ní Ghríofa

IN ÉINEACHT
I gcead d'Alice Maher

Rugadh le hubh mé –
blaosc bhán a scoilt, lá, a d'fhág
gearrcach bídeach i mo lámh.

Gormghlas, bog
an t-éan a d'fhás aníos liom,
gualainn le gob, crúb le cos.
D'aon ghuth a chanamar
is ba bhinn ár bport,

ach anocht, níl eadrainn
ach an tost. Clúmhach
an t-ualach, cleiteach an tocht.

Ná scaoil an tsnaidhm.

Ná lig leis an gcorp.

Go dtite drúcht na hoíche orainn,
go dteipe ar mo ghreim docht,
is mar seo a bheidh againne, againne beirt.

Paddy Bushe

ÉANLAITH NA CÓIVIDE
do Sheán Mac a' tSíthigh

Agus na deich mbliana is trí scór gafa tharam
Le bliain nó dhó anois, táim neadaithe dá réir

Inár dtigh ar bhruach na faille. Riamh ní fhaca
Fíor spéire is farraige chomh lomfhírinneach,

Ná níor thuigeas i gceart cé chomh hionraic
Is atá cloch, carraig is trá. Le teileascóp nua,

Dírím caol díreach ar ghobadán ag fuirseadh
Ar imeall taoide, amhail nach mbeadh aon

Trá eile ar domhan le bheith ag freastal uirthi,
Ná cinnteacht gealaí, ná séasúr, ná rabharta.

Gheibhim freisin cead isteach i nead brosnach
Atá crochta ar dhreap faille tamaillín siar uaim

Go bhfeicim cé chomh geal leis an bhfiach dubh
Is atá a chuid gearrcach féin, fiú agus m'ainmse

Agus ainm gach éinne beo ina leabhar dubh,
Leabhar nach bhfuil radharc air. Má mhairim

Fada go leor, seans go dtiocfaidh sé chugam
Port éin amháin a aithint thar phort éin eile,

Port ceiliúrtha a aithint thar phort rabhaidh
Agus port ealta a aithint thar phort éin chorr.

Tharlódh, fiú, go dtiocfaidh caint don gcéirsigh
Agus Gréigis, ar mh'anam, don lon dubh bhreá.

Is má bhím, ar deireadh, inniúil ar a gcanúint,
Seans go ndéanfad beart de réir a mbriathar.

Aibreán-Meitheamh, 2020

Stiofán Ó hIfearnáin

BOUDICCA

Ní fada ó bhí sí sa chath cois Fleet:
cuardaíonn na seandálaithe rian éigin di,
gach uair a thosaíonn na *digs*.

Nach bhfuil crosbhóthar
a muintire áit éigin sa chré
faoi thraenacha Islington?

Chonac beirt ag imirt fichille
faoi scáth an Tate:
cath úr á fhearadh acu,
cois Thames.

Eaglaisí Wren ag goint ar íor na spéire –
smúdáin na banríona áit éigin faoin talamh.

Mary Shine Thompson

CODE WORDS

Caitríona Ní Chléirchín, translations by Peter Fallon, *The Talk of the Town* (The Gallery Press, 2020), €11.95.

Caitríona Ní Chléirchín's poetic credentials were secured when her first poetry collection, *Crithloinnir* (Coiscéim), won the Oireachtas Prize for New Writers in 2010. Her reputation was consolidated when *An Bhrídeach Sí* (Coiscéim, 2014) was awarded the 2015 Michael Hartnett Prize. Her adroit, often feminist, literary critiques are widely published. However, such are the vicissitudes of writing in a minority language that it was not until her poems appeared in *Calling Cards* (The Gallery Press, 2018), an anthology of younger Irish-language writers, that the verve of her sustained achievement reached a wide readership. Now, with *The Talk of the Town*, she has attained the prestigious milestone of a selected volume, a judicious sweep of a life's work translated by Peter Fallon.

Among the hallmarks of Ní Chléirchín's work are her skill at making the ordinary resonant, her control of the minor key of melancholy, and her glorious lyricism. She has that stilly, greeny capacity for capturing nature at its most serene, reminiscent of Patrick Kavanagh or Patrick Deeley. Such snatches of luminous tranquillity are evident in, for example, 'Clapsholas i nGort na Móna' / 'Duskus, Gortmoney', and are all the more remarkable in a collection that constantly navigates contested boundaries.

Perhaps the speaker's apologia and the collection's fulcrum is the title poem, 'Cogarnach' / 'The Talk of the Town'. The poem begins: 'Uaireanta tuirsím / de bheith i mo bhean' ('From time to time I just / get tired of being a woman'). It embodies many of the collection's preoccupations: secrecies, psychological strains, the straitjackets of gendered identity, and the ever-present spectre of that shape-changer, translation. The rendering of 'cogarnach' (whispering, conspiring), as 'the talk of the town', underlines that inter-linguistic tension.

Writ large is impatience with 'constant / pretendings, / charades / and the concealment of things', of female experience. Memorable are the book's love poems, always haunting and erotic ('Cuimhne' / 'Remembering' is one), and sometimes damning, as, for example, when they lay bare the poison pearls of an abusive relationship (as in 'Muince' / 'Torc'). The domestic 'Nóiméad ar Maidin' / 'A Moment, One Morning' offers a gentle alternative perspective on living and loving. Like Elizabeth Bishop, Ní Chléirchín has mastered the art of losing love and lovers and turning over a new leaf.

Other poems recuperate historical experiences that have been wilfully displaced, as in the heart-rending 'Scaradh na gCompánach' / 'The Parting of the Ways'. Foreboding haunts Hugh O'Neill's wife at the pivotal historical moment of the flight of the earls, as O'Neill obliges her to 'abandon our son to the grip of English' / 'ár mac a fhágáil faoi láimh an Ghaill'.

A further series of poems addresses the violations implicit in border crossings, whose routines and routine terrors were second nature during the Troubles. A poem like 'Moill' / 'Hold Up' graphically plots each humiliation and outrage as border officials line children against a wall and interrogate their mother in a *Shed mór* near Aughnacloy. 'Trasnú na Teorann' / 'Border Crossing' concludes that, within earshot of border posts, 'Ba bhinn béal ina thost' / 'The sweetest sound was silence'.

The sounds of silence are everywhere discernible, most notably in 'Fírinne' / 'The Whole Truth', an elegy for language, for words deadened, frozen, locked up. Particularly mourned are 'focla rúnda', rendered here as 'code words'. One apprehension of 'focla rúnda' is that they conceal dangerous resistance, similar to the mantles that outraged the poet-coloniser Edmund Spenser. These 'focla rúnda' are keys to ending a linguistic lockdown.

Ní Chléirchín's minimalism is a strategic, voluntary act of self-preservation. It implies finding ways of speaking parallel to the dominant semiotic code. By mining the physical reality of women's experience, she inserts herself into the company of Ní Dhomhnaill, Boland, and McGuckian. Adopting the marginalised Irish language is a further act of defiance against the normalising (codification) of experience. The movement towards silence can be creative, productive, and even necessary, as both Beckett and Yeats (I have 'Long-Legged Fly' in mind) indicate.

The Talk of the Town is predicated on contradictions: the Irish version of Emyvale, Ní Chléirchín's home town, is Scairbh na gCaorach, meaning the shallows fording the river where sheep congregate; as such, it embodies possibilities that crossing borders imply. That the physical identity embedded in the Irish toponyms is lost in translation is not lost on Ní Chléirchín. Breaking silence presents a female dilemma: how to express the uncertain, the contradictory, the unthinkable. The paradox of 'Fírinne' / 'The Whole Truth', which writes out the failure of language, is therefore inescapable. Underlying it is the vulnerability of identity and the traumas inscribed on the female body and on the landscape.

A dual-language text such as *The Talk of the Town* is de facto two volumes under one title. Ní Chléirchín's transfigurer, Peter Fallon, is an accomplished poet and experienced translator: in 2004 he took on the might of Virgil's *Georgics* with what Bernard O'Donoghue called 'exemplary precision', and followed it in 2018 with a version of Hesiod's *Works and Days*. He is also *The Talk of the Town*'s publisher and a farmer, and shares Ní Chléirchín's elegiac sensibility and respect for Kavanagh's rural landscapes and poetry.

Fallon implicitly accepts that perfect congruence between languages is impossible, and opts to remain faithful to the sense of the originals, though not the form. He makes his own of poems by introducing subtle, elegant stanzas, as in the delicate 'A Moment, One Morning'. The aesthetic impact of 'In the Middle of the Day' is as intense as that of 'Meán Lae, ag Uaigh an Chaomhánaigh', evoking not only the luminous serenity of a memorial ceremony at Kavanagh's grave, but also Kavanagh's presiding presence. Fallon used his formal licence to good effect in translating 'corcairghorm' (the colour violet) as 'orangy' ('Gealach na gCoinleach' / 'Harvest Moon'). Confusion gives way when the reader recognises the clever play on the shape of '-orcairgh-'.

Fallon is adept too at deploying rural colloquialisms reminiscent of Ní Chléirchín's 'caint na ndaoine': 'since God knows when' is surely right for 'le fada'. His divergences from that path, therefore, are significant. Translating 'amharcaim amach' (literally, 'I look out') as 'I plenish my sight' enables him to shape 'Craobh Liath' into a fine haiku; it is an example of Fallon making his own of the original.

Fallon encounters a mammoth obstacle, in that the translation process necessarily intensifies the loss that is one of Ní Chléirchín's thematic concerns. This is exemplified in, for example, 'Chuaigh Mé do Do Lorg' / 'I Went Out to Find You'. Here, a complex historical, pastoral narrative is rooted in a series of Irish-language toponyms, but this enriching, contextualising sub-narrative is unreproduceable in English. There's a world of historical difference between Caisleán Ghlas Locha and its translation, Castle Leslie.

The paradox of a male poet – Ní Chléirchín's dual-language publisher to boot – translating the linguistically embodied female experience adds what Aifric Mac Aodha called a 'perplexing gendered twist' (in her introduction to *Calling Cards*). There is no resolution to that paradox of a male articulating 'focla rúnda'. Furthermore, the centralising shift implicit in the anthologising process and in the landmark 'selected' volume, steer Ní Chléirchín away from border territories close to her heart. But other gifts have followed, for such loss abundant recompense. This is 'a field of bright // gold'.

Kathy Tynan
Proud and Strong, All Day Long, 2017
Oil on canvas
90 x 90 cm

Kathy Tynan
Was Low the Moon and High the Wind, 2018
Oil on canvas
100 x 90 cm

Kathy Tynan
All Of Old, 2017
Oil on canvas
90 x 90 cm

Kathy Tynan
Curry Club, 2017
Oil on canvas
59 x 84 cm

Kathy Tynan
Laughter in the blood, 2017
Oil on canvas
70 x 70 cm

Kathy Tynan
Thick and Black Roots of the Stars, 2017
Oil on canvas
70 x 80 cm

Kathy Tynan
This Always Present Light, 2017
Oil on canvas
70 x 60 cm

Kathy Tynan
Over Heavy Seas, 2019
Oil on canvas
80 x 80 cm

https://kathytynan.net/
Instagram: @kathy.tynan

Liam Carson

OF THE SEEN AND UNSEEN, OF SILENCE AND EXILE

Paddy Bushe, *Peripheral Vision* (Dedalus Press, 2020), €12.50.
Paddy Bushe, *Second Sight* (Dedalus Press, 2020) €12.50.
Mícheál Ó hAodha, *Leabhar na nAistear* (Coiscéim, 2017), €8.
Mícheál Ó hAodha, *Leabhar na nAistear II* (Coiscéim, 2019), €7.50.

'But sometimes the artist will lead you / And your amazed eyes where reason / / Absolutely refuses to go', writes Paddy Bushe in 'The Art of Belief'. These lines might sum up what is at work in *Peripheral Vision*, a remarkable collection of ekphrastic poems that focus on the nature of how art deals with that which is seen, and that which is unseen. Here the process of creating art is one of watching, of close attention to what is seen or heard, of what Bushe describes as 'Patient attention to every changing detail' in the poem 'The Artist Among the Mountains', a response to John Singer Sargent's *Portrait of Ambrogio Raffaele*.

These poems found their genesis in a 2015 residency in the Centre Culturel Irlandais in Paris, where Bushe determined to visit art galleries and contemplate street sculpture, then to compose poems not '*about* the various sources', but in response to them. The poems not only touch on visual art; music is as central to his work. What we often have is a chain of artistic links, as in 'Scallop', a poem triggered by a Maggi Hambling sculpture inspired by a Benjamin Britten opera:

> These fluted curves encompass every sound
> The world makes, hinged between sea and sky.
> They hear those voices that will not be drowned.

Bushe plays with concepts of sight and visual impairment, and has spoken of how he himself was 'astounded by what I could now see' when he had cataracts removed. This experience feeds into the collection's title poem, 'Peripheral Vision'. Here a woman named Colly starts to 'see things / After the burial of her daughter'. She tells the narrator of the poem how her peripheral blindness enables her to see that which is magical:

> *The eye-doctor told me I had a kind of blindness*
> *That means I can see the sideways things differently.*
> *You see, I see things that other people can't see.*

Craft is an ongoing concern with Bushe, the need for precision in art. Like the piper he often writes about, Bushe himself goes 'searching for tunings in resonant air'. In 'Workshop', he is inspired by a gallery recreation of the workshop of the sculptor Constantin Brancusi, defining the act of creation as one of perpetual honing or revision:

> ... And to return to be
> Worked on again. The whole thing again.

What's perhaps surprising about *Peripheral Vision* is the extent to which it tackles the darkness of politics and war. In 'An Abundance of Glasses', he writes of a pile of cheap chain-store reading glasses he has accumulated, which remind him of a photograph taken by Polish photographer Stanisław Mucha after the liberation of Auschwitz-Birkenau concentration camp. 'The Sleep of Reason Creates Monsters' is a villanelle, a form Bushe finds useful to 'hammer home a message, suitable for political purposes'. Written on the day of Donald Trump's election in 2016, it not only responds to the Goya etching of its title, but also borrows a card-playing trope from an Aogán Ó Rathaille poem:

> Succession now falls on the fool and the gambler,
> Jokers and knaves have trumped the royal game.
> Prophecy's black candles cast a deep shadow.

In 'A Postcard from Knossos', Bushe writes of Dedalus 'being wary / Of high flyers, of the big splash, of playing / To the gods' – and there's a sense in which his poems unfurl gently, without fuss. He refers to 'the music of what happens' (no doubt a nod to Seamus Heaney's 'Song'). But if his poems do not 'have notions of themselves', they have a terrific cumulative power that can only be described as symphonic. The Holocaust surfaces repeatedly, as do images of battlefield slaughter and carrion crows; there is the siege of Leningrad, and the driven music of war pipes.

Peripheral Vision's closing section includes the poem 'Amergin's Ship'. It of course references 'The Song of Amergin', in which the poet Amergin seeks 'To be the land and the land's creatures / To be the stones raised in commemoration'. Which brings us to *Second Sight*, a new selection of his work in Irish, with his own English translations. In 'Carraig Taibhrimh' (or 'Stone Dreaming'), there is the lovely couplet:

> Déantar carraig díom,
> Carraig taibhrimh.

> ('Let me be stone / Stone dreaming.')

The Amergin myth is brilliantly riffed on by Bushe in 'Coiscéim Aimhirghin' ('The Amergin Step'), and in 'Freagra Scéine ar Aimhirghin' ('Scéine's reply to Amergin'):

> Más loch ar mhá thú
> > Raghad go tóinn poill ionat
> Más tú rún na héigse
> > Mise na naoi mBéithe agat

('If you are a lake in the plain / I will plumb your very depths. / If you are the essence of poetry / I am all of your muses.')

Bushe is powerfully drawn to liminal zones or landscapes, particularly those threatened by man, as in 'Giorria Artach' ('Arctic Hare'):

> Tásc ná tuairisc níl agamsa le coicíos
> Ar an saol mór ná ar chinnithe na bhfear
> A labhrann le Dia is a labhrann Dia leo
> Roimh scaoileadh na mbuamaí, roimh an gol san ár.

('For two weeks now, I've had neither sight nor sound / Of the big world, nor of the decrees of men / Who speak to God and to whom God speaks / Before the bombs' release, the weeping in the slaughter.')

In 'Búireadh' ('Bellowing'), a melting glacier is imagined as an animal, given life, and as it melts and cracks it sounds 'Mar a bheadh tréad i bpéin' ('Like a herd in pain'). In this book's last section, he returns to the landscapes of the Iveragh peninsula and the islands of the Skelligs. His poetry is replete with references to Irish mythology, to the Fianna and 'The Book of Invasions', and a landscape where the placenames themselves contain story and song. In 'Oileánú' ('Islanding') he imagines himself as looking into 'ceo' (mist or fog), 'Mar sheilimide éigin farraige' ('Like some sea-snail or other'), a monk-like scribe shrinking into himself, with his pencil, capturing the landscape he is part of.

If Bushe's poetry is rooted in ancient landscapes, Mícheál Ó hAodha's poems in the two-volume collection *Leabhar na nAistear* are concerned with a people uprooted from their native land and living in exile – more specifically those who took the boat ('an Bád Bán') to Britain in search of a better life in the 1950s. These are the men who worked on the building sites of London, Hull, Leeds, and Peterborough, and who built the M1 and M6 motorways; and the women who became nurses or worked in cafés and bars. It is estimated that half of all Irish people born in the 1930s emigrated during this decade, the majority to Britain.

It's the world of novelist Dónall Mac Amhlaigh's *Deoraithe* (*Exiles*), which has recently been translated into English by Ó hAodha. He has also translated Seosamh Mac Grianna's *Mo Bhealach Féin* (as *This Road of Mine*). These are writers who in very different ways address themes of travel and alienation, but also the failures of an Irish state that abandoned its people. This bitter reality is the heart of the poem 'Mise Éire':

> ar shroiseadh bharr an tsléibhe dom
> thosaigh an ghrian ag dul faoi sa spéir fholamh
> smaoinigh mé fúthu siúd go léir a cailleadh
> ar son na talún sin,
> ansin dheineas dearmad orthu

Homage is paid to Mac Amhlaigh in the poem 'Aislingí'. Like many of the poems in these two collections, it is a haunted poem, with 'tost' ('silence') at its heart. Words are gathered into silence like a railway line vanishing into the distance:

> imíonn an líne iarnróid as amharc
> 'nós focail á gcuachadh ag an tost
> an ráille traenach folamh
> á ghabháil ag an bhfómhar

Sometimes the poems consist of snatches of conversation, a few lines from a letter, or recalled pub chatter. Ó hAodha often talks of 'an domhan sa dán' ('the world in the poem'), and he builds up the world of his exiled characters through an accumulative weave of images and themes. Again and again there are sightings of travel bags, mice scurrying in shabby lodgings, imagined maps on bedroom walls, there are trains leaving and arriving. The recurring snow of his poetry links past, present, and future. Sometimes the snow hides darkness, as in 'Ag Fanacht ar an Leoraí Oibre' ('Waiting for the Work Lorry'):

> ag seasamh sa sneachta, ag seasamh i dtost
> an toitín deireanach á shú síos go bun
> smaointe grá is díoltais, smaointe díoltais is mó

Ó hAodha's poems might best be described as micro-poems. They are short, stripped to the bone, often haiku-like. They are deeply suggestive in their condensed lyricism. These are poems in which little things ('nithe beaga') reveal a lot – 'nithe beaga a bhraithim uaim / an ghaoth a shéid oíche aréir'. Ó hAodha's poetry may be brief in form, but it contains marvellous multitudes.

Nick Laird

VALENCY

Robbed, I kept on looking for
what I'd lost and came on
something like it left in a hedge,

and picked it up, and hurried off,
and held it close but it felt never
quite like mine – in parts too soft,

and here too hard, and with this
smell of foreignness, even now
as I lay on my back and watched

the clouds wrap us in a shroud.
As particular words disappear
from the language one forgets

how to have certain sensations.
All do not all things well.
The day breaks like a plank.

It's so relentless being one's self
I want to claw the skin off
and climb out now. It is endless

until it does and you become
tar; onions; a sheepshank knot;
a carburettor rusting in the grass.

Nick Laird

SHEEP'S HEAD

I opened the door before on the light and the light
rain falling on the water, on the roof of the hire car,
on the field and its three cattle waiting out the weather,

and a mobile of gannets twisting over the crib
of the harbour – buffeted, angling, tacking bright sails
to the gusts of light rain coming off the stroppy Atlantic.

The light was the light of nowhere – emanating equally
off the mountain, the gateposts, a colourless sea –
to be absorbed completely by the ruined pewter sky

where the gannets perfect gannet-ness, practising
an exact control before collapse; the contraptions
of themselves, all the sheer extended apparatus

of their empire, contracting to the point, to the fall,
to this choreographing of a series of vanishings
that stipple the dark roil. And there is no mail

but there is a sizeable orb spider abseiling off
the letterbox pursued by a chain of raindrops
suent as the row of buoys set out for the mussel lines,

a few tangents to the circle of the fish farm,
the open-topped cage net John Murphy waited
nearly four years to replace after the last big storm.

The light rain darkens the Goat's Path and the lane
down to the Cove, an abrupt bite in the cliff, the ribbed
concrete jetty and the big ring of the mooring rusting

into nothing, into shrieks of gulls and a brass plaque
speckled with light rain embedded in the black rock
where Farrell, spinning for mackerel, got taken by a wave.

In Durrus at the Church of Ireland the light rain is falling
on the yew, falling on the ground where the routine is
granted its beautiful due and a raindrop ached off the tip

of a leaf when they planted Farrell in the ground,
ground which has always been holy, if only for the reason
that the yew is growing there. Every now and then

an unprisoning god will appear in the realm of things,
and as with all gods must borrow the shapes of the place,
and what happened with John Murphy's fish farm was

the storm struck hard and there was nothing where net was
before and out of a rip in the continuum poured the salmon,
a hundred ton of them as one thrashing and liveried mass –

nosing separately downwards in thousands to edgeless depths,
I guess, since it was October and I was here at my carrel,
stopping late for lunch, taking the stairs down two at a time

to Washington Square, mid-poem, heading every direction,
while the guy is playing a Haydn sonata on that baby grand
he wheels out every morning with some friend into the sun.

Luke Morgan

ZAMBIA

Nobody move. Boyd, our driver,
hand daring towards the rifle on his belt.
No windows. Hardly a roof.
We were dead.
She placed so deftly alongside us
it was as though the sky was on a conveyor
and she, perfectly still.
She stared at me. Everything
got swimmy – like when we were kids
and Jake threw a rock at the back
of my head.
Look. I showed him my crimson hand,
in stupid awe of its stickiness
between my fingers, its persistence
in every tiny tract of my skin,
and he, face crumpling,
certain he had killed me,
running to the end of the garden
to await his lifelong punishment
of silence.
The lioness opened her mouth
and licked that blood from my fingers.
Her tongue was warm
as a nurse's voice.
Then, almost bored, she turned back
to her cubs.
I touched her saliva to the back of my head
where the hair has stopped growing
and remembered the soft instruction –
Sleep on your side for a few days,
don't scratch, and try not to get caught
out in the rain.

Jessica Traynor

DAD CARS

Down into the mine we drive them,
leave them to rust into living rock.
The red Cortina bleached pink
headlights flicking on, off,
against quartz.

Then the Morris Minor,
a shadow at the pit's base –
we shake our heads, laugh
at how the floor fell out
on the motorway.

The aspirational Triumph,
its bonnet cop-car blue,
the chrome Dad loved
weeping rust into the water table.

And the breakup Volvo
with its denial of sex,
like a divorcee dedicating
themselves to the worship
of their own boxy body,

the car that won't collapse,
that will sit in this cavern
sugar-coated with calcite,
till stalactites candle it
to a pipe organ.

I promise him: some day
I'll bury him here
in the oil-soaked sand,
a wing-mirror in each hand,

a battery block beneath his head,
and the last, unstolen car radio
singing
            in the mine's heart.

Alyson Favilla

DID SAPPHO EVER TRIPLE-TEXT?
after Marilyn Hacker

so one night I get drunk
read all of Sappho
and decide my love needs a new name

a text is a text, is a body
imagine I am codifying
for the very first time

(did Sappho ever triple-text?)
the crush of adoration
shamelessly I'll fragment her

anoint her with absurdities
spread them in her lap and
fan a deck of dedications like

pale-throated one / one
bright with desire
adorned with goldenrod and ivy ...

but who hasn't burned like this?
what naked letter curls against the shape of her shape
like a girl beside the fragment of a girl?

Alyson Favilla

TRUE CRIME

My love replays the murders
as told by two women, friends.

Their clear voices describe
the body: explicit, unhidden;

the bruises, marks, suspicions
pressed into the skin like flowers

between the pages of a book,
the horror: finding what was left to find.

Gently, they share the mortuary details,
the motive (cautious speculation),

as if a motive were possible, as if
the killer had not merely excised

with the greatest possible violence
the wish some poor girl embodied:

to live and keep living.
This is the source of dread,

not the new pandemic
but the silence that recently prevails

when both the episode is paused and
the keen whirr of the old machine she

has commandeered for mask-making,
crafting all she can from what she's found,

as if, despite what she's heard,
all that might be saved might be saved,

if only love would intervene.

Paul Batchelor

THE PARASITE
  5 May 1640

Algernon Percy, 10th Earl of Northumberland,
naked as innocence before the mirror,
ties his necklace – fine blue silk, adorned
with an enamel-gold medallion of St George
lancing the dragon: very good! – and then
in a dramatic gesture only I observe
sweeps his riding cloak about his shoulders.
The left side bears a star-shaped aureole
emblazoned in silver thread. There. Admirably done.

One hour from now the Privy council will request
that he, newly appointed Lord Protector, raise
an army against the rebel Scots. My host –
Commander-in-Chief and the King's favourite, yes,
but also scrutinant of his coffers and flat broke –
gives me a run-through of his stalling tactics:
To raise tax on your majesty's prerogative
will only meet a fraction of the cost
and fail as surely as the last war did – no, no!

It's time. We are accompanied to Whitehall
by footmen, coachmen, and postilions
all liveried in blue silk with silver wire,
the Garter round a crescent: his heraldic badge;
to think – the pity of it! – he must risk all this
persuading His Majesty to compromise ...
Steel-rimmed carriage wheels rattle, pebbles scatter,
London turns in its bed to face the wall
and my host tries once more to hammer it out:

Majesty, might it be politic to affect
a superstition on the need for parliament's
moral – that is, financial – backing when at war?
That sounds more like it. Alighting on Queen's Road
he takes the steps two at a time
allowing the slightest of smiles to play
about his lips. A hopeful gleam of first light
flashes back at him from the paving stones
and he feels a passing dizziness come over him ...

Inside, my host is busy with confections,
a crucible in which I'm gently crushed,
part of the soup, part of the recipe
that makes up Algernon's compendium.
Since the blood meal when we met six days ago
I've shadowed him close as an apprentice.
Right now I'm gazing through the jelly of his eyes
as through stained glass. I see a cat-faced man,
a half-smile glutted with contempt: the king.

Suddenly I will declare myself with seizures,
enlargement of the liver and the spleen,
convulsions and religious mania,
keeping my host from the field and the court.
And should historians of the future ask
If Percy had prevailed, might civil war
have been prevented? – I will answer that
my kind, preferring time to history,
seriously incline towards a longer view.

Jane Clarke

HER FIRST

We wait on grey plastic chairs
with the other births, deaths and marriages.

The sun tries to shine
through narrow, frosted windows.

Close to lunchtime
the registrar ushers us into her office –

stacks of files on every surface
look set to topple.

She murmurs *You're my first,*
and reads out the regulations

as if translating a foreign script,
then shuffles through papers,

studies the stapler on her desk
and reads them again. When we tell her

we've been together twenty years
she stops searching for a biro,

meets our eyes and smiles,
It'll be a beautiful day.

Victoria Kennefick

ALTERNATIVE MEDICINE

I am here to heal, to confess to that darkness
standing in front of my eyes when I open them,

that food squirms with maggots as if alive,
that I have shut my mouth to everything but words.

The therapist taps my shoulders, my head, my knees,
tells me I was a nun once, very strict.

This makes sense; I know how cleanly I like
to punish myself. Also, a Celtic priestess,

I hope I had red hair, that I ate men
like air, all that jazz.

She moves to my forehead; her fingers drum
on my skin. There were two of you, she says.

My body remembers in a jolt, the guilt
black and endless. It is a tunnel.

No, it is someone else's shadow. Almost like mine.
A twin, poor thing. In my mother's womb

I consumed this sibling, she says, like I gnaw
at my flesh now, my body feeding on whatever scrap.

You didn't do it, she says. *I know I did,*
I know I did. My little twin, one of us had to go.

Victoria Kennefick

SECOND COMMUNION

The altar boy tinkles the bell.
Father Madden enters, his chasuble fluid as milk;
a shaft of sunlight pierces the Christ embroidered in tinsel –

that feeling
(not hunger)

My mother, in her mink coat, smells of the expensive perfume my father buys
in duty-frees. He is next to her in tweed, then my little sister – a frill.
Father Madden reads a gospel, in my tummy a throb –

unwrap it
(not thirst)

Burying my face deep into the pelt of my mother's coat, musk tussles
with the sweet incense of prayer. My head rises as the priest lifts the host –
I see the cut of it, that tiny moon –

I don't want to eat
(any body)

If I eat Jesus will he want to eat me?
Think on that, not the chalice sloshing with blood. Soon it will be time
to stutter up the aisle, open my mouth and be fed.

Kelly Michels

LOCKDOWN:

       from *lock*, an old Germanic word
meaning *to fasten*, a fastening mechanism, a turn
of phrase changing according to the preposition
to determine people or things, as in, *to lock in*
pertaining to people, or *to lock up*, pertaining
to things or the chamber itself, i.e. to lock up the house
or to lock up valuables, in North American usage
to lock up refers to prisoners, i.e. my mother was
locked up, meaning my mother was a thing, which is
not surprising, she stopped being real a long time ago,
but now that she is dead, it is a problem of direction,
whether to look up or down when speaking, and from this
comes the second part of a compound word, *down*:
an adverb meaning descent, or a noun, meaning
a bundle of feathers to keep us warm as arctic birds,
and when taken together, *lockdown*, a term first used
in the 70s when referring to inmates in prisons or
patients in psychiatric hospitals during riots,
was a method to keep them safe from themselves,
snug as small caged birds strip searched, chanting
Attica, Attica, into the hollow, point-blank dark,
and later in the 90s, the term came to refer to schools
and children, meaning a boy walks down the hall
with a Glock 19, Mossberg 500, or a Smith & Wesson
his parents gave him for Christmas, and you have
fifteen seconds or less to barricade the door, jump away
from the window, call your mother, hide under a desk,
hello, can you hear me? and hope for the best
like a snail on barbed wire

and now in 2020, we watch the clouds multiply
as if the sky was contagious, and we, too,
learn not to move, like a child stuffed in a closet
waiting for the footsteps to fade, meaning
it is no longer safe to touch the living, no longer safe
to say goodbye to our dead, we peer at them
through dirty windows instead, mouthing the words,
hello, can you hear me? as they take their last
breath: meaning, grief is a lost key to a house we are

not allowed to enter, like a doorway during the bubonic
plague: *Lord have mercy* written over a cross in red paint
where the lymph nodes of the sick swelled like black balloons,
and centuries later, the Victorians called it Black Death
with their penchant for the perfect little obsidian dress,
and nearly 200 years afterward, a new millennium of purples
and pinks, a virus, heavy as a disco ball, bright as badly dyed
Easter eggs cracking across every hemisphere
until even the Pope grows afraid, the frayed sound
of a helicopter drifting from one hospital to the next,
like incense trembling through an empty basilica,
while angels hover in white plastic gowns
their faces shielded and blurred
placing body after body into the earth,
like small pale bulbs knitted through the dirt,
glowing like starlight as if the world were upside down
and we spend our day praying for resurrection
the clock dripping toward evening, my neighbour
clumsily strumming *House of the Rising Sun*
on his guitar, for hours, outside in the rain,
as I belt out the words in my head, *Oh mother,*
tell your children, not to do what I have done
stay where you are, don't walk, don't run,
this will only last a little while, and when
all this is over, I swear to god, things will change;
when all this is over, we will hang our heads in kindness
or in shame.

Maia Elsner

FRONTISPIECE

```
so beautiful          in brushstrokes              Bathsheba
in the Louvre         my grandfather's             loss frames
the letter in her         hands –                  her beloved
destroyed      ordered to the front line in order      to die
his loved ones                                          also
Ryszard                                           on the train
Bruno                                            buying bread
Paris is                                        a lonely place
to seek asylum                                 at every corner
PTSD                                              memory of
Cecilia                                         Cecilia again
taken                                            King David
wanted her                                            & so
spilled blood                                         later
my grandfather                                   learns she dies
in Belzec                                     what they did to her
in Belzec                                          here in Paris
he sees her                                        in every face
along the Seine                                   as Rembrandt
imagining                                           Bathsheba
finds his own                                         beloved
& paints her                                     my grandfather
seeks                                                 an end
each day plans                                    the final day
& ends up            in the Louvre again         tears spilling
as he looks      at this painting of someone       so loved
a statement that     there is love still          & perhaps
it might be              worth it                 to stay alive
```

Dermot Bolger

THE UNGUARDED MOMENT

At sixty, the hardest part of going back to being a poet
Are the terms and conditions in the zero-hours contract.

Novels may be ground out on dull Tuesday afternoons,
But you must let poems ambush you when least expected,

On a street corner or midway down a supermarket aisle,
In the unguarded moment when you find yourself writing

Without even being aware that you are trying to write;
When a single thought sparks with a jolt of electricity

That short circuits all cognizance of what task you were at
And ignites the dry undergrowth in your subconscious

That has lain dormant through long months of drought,
Waiting for a wind to blow up, for a random stranger

Lost in thought on a parched headland of yellow gorse,
To carelessly toss away their smouldering cigarette butt.

Mary Noonan

TIME TRAVELLERS

At Carcassonne, snow is stopping flights,
so we scurry back to the holiday flat.
Already strange, the space has been sealed
in dust, the prints and dents of human bodies
levelled. In the doorway, we hear a gasp –
the ghosts of our yesterday selves, sitting
at the table and raising the Christmas wine,
faces glowing in the light of a poppy candle,
do a quick double-take at this rude eruption
from the future. We barge in, shake out
the sheets and watch the spectres dissolve,
mingle with motes in the stale air.
Then a new smell prangs our nostrils:
three spring hyacinths, that yesterday were
fat bulbs in their trough, have bloomed into
blazing torches for lighting a way through snow.
Or three admirals on the prow of today,
breasting the future in dazzling whites.

Dean Browne

PINBALL
            for Matthew Sweeney

He let the oxygen mask slip
from the crow's nest of stubble
so I leant in closer, to catch
that he didn't want a headstone –
no wings, no spidery gothic script –
instead, an old pinball machine
should mark the place of his grave.
He liked the plink under his thumbs;
he talked bumpers, flippers, kickers,
forbidden tilts, 'shooting for the moon',
how a ball knocked out of bounds
might come back, Lazarus, and win.
I saw tournaments among the tombs,
a horsebox paused by the fresh earth,
a generator, set up to the side
under that knuckle of hill in Donegal.
He inserts the first cold coins
by the yew trees, under the moon,
pulls the plunger – flashing outlanes
bop and spark against the marble,
focusing names and dates,
gilt epitaphs and stone angels
watching hi-scores rack up.
I know before the night is out
his initials will join the wizards.

Dean Browne

AIDE-MÉMOIRE

A goat has been following me for hours. There is a sign
hung around his neck that reads NEVER FORGET.
That's not very original I think but I'll see where it leads.
"I have no grá for you goat," I say, and clap my hands, say, "Go!"
His goat eye asks if I am half-cracked. "Grand," I say,
and keep walking. He follows at a discreet distance, beard
jigging crooked as he jaws blankly at some grass he cropped
years ago, I suppose. What am I meant to remember?
Leaves are smeared on the street, a salad of dragged newspaper.
Nobody appears to notice what is following me. I detour
into a dive bar, roll a cigarette, drink a double whiskey
and try to decide where, if anywhere, all this might connect.
Goat stands by the door, NEVER FORGET dripping to the tiles.
I watch wet leaves fibrillate outside the window, think
of the small, delicate feather on this morning's egg. Leaf, light,
leaf, light. Quick silverfish glimpses of a freedom that spooks
on approach. The goat chews on, relentless. I mash my cigarette,
touch my ear, and it comes off.

Michael Dooley

PENINSULA AT NIGHT

He swore he had seen her drink
from the teat of a cow,
and she was a hare then, or a witch.
A sea stack pops its head above the swell;
lights again in the rear-view mirror.
Loop Head roads wind in narrow buckles
like hawthorn, or chine of dying sheep –
horses could not pull from him
the thought of her.
In the doorway, she listens
against the quietness:
the Atlantic
bubbling like a sleeping child;
stone teething through soil;
a *snitch, snitch, snitch,*
of cattle grazing in darkness;
the hinge of a gate on a windless night;
the questioning of herself;

a low growl from the dog.

Kate Quigley

GALWAY OYSTER FESTIVAL

The wet kelp rot of the docks
seeping across the city,
baked by that rare week

without rain,
every hotel & upmarket eatery
touting their stake;

champagne to mask
the salt commonality of
mollusc, bivalve,

the dark peat malt
of stout to drown out
the sweet pale tang.

He stands at the intersection
between Shop Street & St Nicholas',
tracksuit bottoms cuffed

into white socks,
two buckets, no ice,
brimmed with the blue-grey

corrugate of sea, little huts
of brine & secret flesh,
his slender boy-arms

working fast, shucking
with rough fluency,
one eye cocked for the cops,

the slap-pat exchange
of coin & shell
with gormless Americans,

he thumbs his knife,
squints over each brailled
glut of fortune,
each raw house of star.

James Conor Patterson

FEAR, UNCERTAINTY & DOUBT

The chip on your shoulder is strange weather.
A growth like snow, or a pustule of hail,
after a freak storm which ruins summer
and gets people talking about *insured peril*.
In May, the NTMA issues a bond
to the tune of €1.5 billion.
A few of your pals graduate then abscond
to England or Australia, and bureaus
up & down the country drive a roaring trade.
Everything's fucked. In September, S&P
announce that *Ireland is at risk of downgrade*
and a friend of a friend walks into the sea.
Someone on Facebook remarks on your likeness.
Your heartbeat remembers: *Cri-sis. Cri-sis.*

Jonathan Greenhause

BEACONS OF LIGHT

"The sea will claim what belongs to the sea," says my son
at age 6. We're steering
a rusted fishing vessel in the middle
of the Atlantic. Cattle soar above us
in a jetliner heading to pastureland. "The sea's
just another word for oblivion," says my son
as he reels in another refugee
& gently hugs her, wraps her in the emergency
Mylar blanket. He pulls out
a cellphone, activates
Google Translate, & the woman's Arabic becomes
"Your President is a vulture with a hunger
for its own eggs," as she pleads
to be taken somewhere else, maybe
Canada. The other refugees
nod their heads, tell tall tales of a distant
Manitoba. "The sea will devour our beacons of light
in their death throes," says my son
as he leaps overboard, dives beneath
the sky's reflection, saves
a small shivering boy barely distinguishable from himself.

Kathleen Jamie

MY PARENTS

In the hallway of our 50s semi
my folks stand, radiant,
because, I say, You're dead now.
You know that, don't you? Here,
come forward; Dad you too,
just a few steps nearer the mirror
framed above your half-moon
telephone table, and side by side
see how your faces glow
now you're no longer alive
behind the rattly door
that opens to the path which you,
Mum, lined so artfully
with sea-worn pebbles
brought home from our holiday beach,
then the street, where the neighbour's lad's
still stripping down his purple Cortina,
and a gang of us bairns is playing
dodgey-ball, 'cause it's a Saturday
so when you shout us in
we'll plead: *Aw, just a bit longer,*
longer, please, till late.

Kathleen Jamie

OUR GARDEN

Are we finished now,
done with piling up on this Earth?
– leaving the debris: slabs, slates
that might yet come in useful,
a stack of bricks stamped
Darngavel or *Bourtreehill*
– kilns long cooled out of their red-heat –
slowly smoored under
ruderal grasses and sprays of herb-robert,
and a rain-filled Belfast sink:
a pinch of duckweed, a couple of sunken stones
and look, its enamel rim's
become a frog-resort –
three attend today, the green-
gold sharp-hipped frog-monarch,
the thumb-length twins, one
resting its chin on the other. Nine
is the record one August afternoon ...
Where do they go otherwise?
Squeezed amongst the rubble
which will still be heaped here
after we are dust. Today they bask,
eyes apparently unseeing
until our fiend-shadows
pass over them
                    then they jump.

Emily S Cooper

FATHER FIGURES: CONJURING MICHAEL DONAGHY

I came to Michael Donaghy's poetry eight years after his death in 2004. I immediately became transfixed by the idea that Donaghy and my late father must have met at a trad session in London. I know that sounds bizarre – my father had died of cancer a few months before and grief does strange things to your mind – but the idea isn't actually as far-fetched as it seems. Both Donaghy and my father were trad musicians who lived in North London in the late Eighties. Donaghy had moved to London from Chicago after growing up in New York with Irish parents. My parents had moved there from Dublin via Libya; my father had left Belfast at eighteen and was determined never to go back. Donaghy played the bodhrán, tin whistle, and flute, my father the banjo and mandolin, so they could conceivably have played during the same sessions. They were both young men (born in the same year, 1954) recently transplanted from other places, holding onto a national identity fragmented by war and geography. And now they were both dead, so I could never find out if they really had ever met. But this fantasy imbued Donaghy's poetry with a sense of familiarity, almost as if he was a family friend whose work I could stake some sort of claim to, despite having no direct connection to it.

As a projected poetic father figure goes, you could do worse than Michael Donaghy. His precision and lightness of touch is matched by the depth and generosity of emotion in his poetry. A master of *Ars Poetica*, Donaghy invites the reader not to read just for content or form, but to engage with the nature of poetry itself. The first poem of *Shibboleth*, Donaghy's debut collection, is 'Machines' and, as an introduction to his work, Donaghy firmly places the harmony of form and content as the central tenet of his poetry, stating that 'The machinery of grace is always simple', and 'As bicyclists and harpsichordists prove / / Who only by moving can balance, / Only by balancing move.' As a young poet, I found this ethos to be fundamental; the notion that the form does not lead but works in a developing coherence with the poem. Having been thrust out into the world through a Catholic Grammar English Literature education, I had always felt constrained by ideas of the definitive nature of poetic conventions. Donaghy (and other poets I discovered once I found myself studying at Goldsmiths), allowed me to relax, to see a poem not as a puzzle to be solved, but something playful and exciting, potentially as intuitive as the emotional engagement you can wordlessly have with music.

I was introduced to Irish poetry through two very distinct streams: the mystical Celtic Twilight of Yeats, and the Troubles poetry of the Belfast Group. I am glad that at this pivotal time I had access to Michael

Donaghy's poetry, which is flavoured by Ireland but not overwhelmed by it. Cultural identity is a strange currency that changes value from hand to hand, and as a young Irish woman in London who – at the time I first read Donaghy – had spent more time off the island than on it, I felt constantly confronted by the pressure to present myself (in person and in my writing) as not only Irish, but a version of Irish that would satisfy an (often English) audience. I was asked in a tutorial whether I had made the choice to deal with the Troubles in my work or not, as if this was a central decision for an Irish writer: either confront it or ignore it. It hadn't occurred to me up until that point that I was an official representative of the politics of the North, and the idea that I should be doing the work to educate those around me didn't sit well. In Donaghy, I found an example of a writer with a multifaceted cultural identity that broadened rather than restricted how he wrote. *Shibboleth*, the collection and the poem, are named for the Hebrew term for a word or phrase that distinguishes a person as part of a group, a marker of belonging that only an insider would know. This preoccupation with belonging resonated with me. In Donaghy I found someone who was also neither here nor there, not enough of a nation to truly pass, but of a sufficient amount to invite scrutiny. For me, the idea of an 'Irish Poetics' was something that I had to work through in order to start saying what I really wanted to say, and Donaghy was a poet who had already been through that and was safely out the other side.

I have discovered that you can listen to Donaghy reading his poetry online. He was known for his live readings and would memorise all of his poems (something I admire but could never manage). He reads with precision, his accent familiar in its inoffensive American tones, the lines are clipped and seem to end suddenly. There is something strange about listening to someone who has died, in a similar way to viewing photographs. It is hard to not notice the unreality, a connection broken from that moment to this. It can be startling if you knew a person well. My mother has kept the same phone since my father died, paying an additional unnecessary cost for an unused land line so that my father's voicemail message remains to this day. It reminds me of the voicemails he used to leave me when I didn't answer the phone, "Hello Emily, this is your father", vaguely ridiculous in their formality. Donaghy's poem 'The Excuse' centres around a hesitant phone call and has the brilliant lines:

> 'My father's sudden death has shocked us all'
> Even me, and I've just made it up ...

As ever, Donaghy balances the unreality of a poem with the reality of the world, and in particular the emotional world, that it comes from. The poem does not replicate a phone call, in the same way that the recordings of Donaghy's voice, or my father's voice, can't really replicate the real thing. But perhaps there is some comfort to be found in a simulacrum.

When someone dies prematurely, it becomes the most notable thing about them. Nearly every essay and article I encounter about Michael Donaghy starts with the same sentiment: Donaghy's early death was a cruel blow to poetry. Even this piece mentions his death in the first line. My father, the other dead person I've mentioned, is defined by his death too. You know practically nothing about him except that he is dead. You should know that he was offensively intelligent: knowledgeable on everything from microbiology to the Latin names of flowers to characters in *Coronation Street* (even though he didn't watch it). He was an incredible cook who would make feasts in a state of rage (which I have inherited) then sit down in complete relaxation and drink a glass of wine with his terrified guests. He was an internationally known scientist and a locally respected pharmacist. He was kind and moral, but also temperamental and never suffered fools. Death has shadowed much of that; when people ask about my parents, it becomes an uncomfortably intimate conversation once you confess that one of them is dead. Luckily, we have Donaghy's writing to provide us with some of the information that his death has obscured. Despite being a confessedly slow writer (he is said to have declared that he only wrote three poems a year), we have three beautiful collections, a fourth posthumous one, and many extraneous poems and critical works that have been collected. It is possible to get something like the essence of a person through their work, not the whole thing, but an impression of their humour and wit and humanity. All of which are present in abundance in Donaghy's writing.

There are a lot of things I have learned from Donaghy's poetry: to end on a line that throws the reader back up to the title as an invitation to read again, to keep your poetry compact, that poetic Easter eggs are fun for both the poet and the more knowledgeable reader (and Donaghy has plenty of Easter eggs in his work), but to hang the poem on something else, to keep it accessible to all, especially in its emotional content. I think this last lesson has been the most important. It's something like the pop-cultural term 'Big Dick Energy'; you can attach all the bells and whistles that you want, spread a poem over a page like poetic Nutella, but the poems that you just trust are good enough, even when they're simple and available, are the ones that will resonate. Nobody really cares if you've read Baudelaire or the complete works of Keats; just as they don't care what grades you got in school or how many times you dropped out. They care if, when they read your work, they can see themselves a little clearer, if the poem clears a bit of space in the mess of their consciousness for the time they spend with it.

In his long poem, 'Black Ice and Rain', Donaghy presents us with a story within a story. A stranger at a party telling his host the tale of a couple he was close with. The high register recalls classic works of nesting dolls; the *Decameron*, or 'My Last Duchess' by Robert Browning, but the content explores a more modern preoccupation: the hollowness of the postmodern habit of art as acquisition rather than craft. The couple end up in a car crash, one dies but the woman (whom the narrator desires) survives, heavily scarred by the accident. In her distress she calls the narrator by her dead lover's name and he takes his opportunity, finally, to sleep with her. This compulsion to project the dead onto available surfaces, be it living people, paintings, or poetry is something we all share. Have you ever had a moment of recognition of a passer-by on the street, only to remember that the person in your mind is already dead? Donaghy is constantly communing with the deceased in his work; his father is mentioned often and he meets the ghost of his uncle who fought and died for the Nationalist cause in the Spanish Civil War, stopping to have a disagreement with him.

I began to write to my father, poems in the second person that discussed his death, or other memories of childhood. Later, I began to write from his perspective, telling the stories he had told me: the night of my birth, the time he saw a man stabbed with a screwdriver in a chip shop, the click of the recorder that tapped our phone when we were living in London in the early Nineties. I also began to give Donaghy cameos, he played the bodhrán in the pub on the night my mother went into labour, he watched as my father and uncle carried bar stools onto the Tube and tried to rent them out to good-looking girls. I decided that if I couldn't be sure if they had met in reality, I could make them meet in my poetry, or at least share the same space.

Martin Malone

ALL THIS HUMAN WORK

Seán Hewitt, *Tongues of Fire* (Jonathan Cape, 2020), £10.
Laurence O'Dwyer, *The Lighthouse Journal* (Templar Poetry, 2020), £10.
Adam Crothers, *The Culture of My Stuff* (Carcanet Press, 2020), £10.99.

A much-heralded debut and two sophomore collections here, and either
I'm easy to please or a fortunate reviewer, because I've rarely been so
content to spend time in such company. Though very different reads,
each book works its distinctive style to remarkable effect, while retaining
the precious ability to convince, move, and amuse. These poets come
with impressive reputations and a slew of awards – something that often
leads the reader to sit back with a sceptical 'come on then, impress me'.
I'm happy to report, they duly oblige.

Seldom does a widely praised debut so fully warrant the hyperbole
surrounding it as *Tongues of Fire*, which gathers about itself critical
verbiage like 'important', 'tour-de-force', and 'triumph', bearing each with
grace. I felt myself in the company of greatness here; the sort to reinvest
one with a sense of just how transcendental poetry can be when it gazes
at nature, life, love, and death with a clear eye, faith in its own possibilities, and a steady craft. The collection doesn't try to reinvent the wheel
for current consumption, nor ostentatiously hitch itself to contemporary
cause; rather, it has the quiet chutzpah to stand in poetry's heartland
and own it for itself. Hewitt writes in the grand traditions of the craft; in
the line of Keats, Hopkins, Hardy, Thomas, Lawrence, Hughes, Plath,
Heaney, and Wordsworth, whose 'impulse from the vernal wood' he re-
works time and again to teach us 'more of man'. With the gay eclogue of
'Dryad', I suppose it could be said he goes back even further, though this
remains a very contemporary collection by virtue of, well, its own time-
less virtues. Its subjects – love, grief, time, family, wandering, that which
is sacred – and the settings – woodland (a *leitmotif* throughout), fields,
edgeland, times of the day or year – are classic fare for the poet and,
consequently, carry a heavy burden of tradition. It is Seán Hewitt's
triumph, then, that he wears all this new and convincingly. Not only
that but he seems to consciously seek out well-trodden ground so as to
traverse it in his own way. The bog body poem 'Old Croghan Man', for
example, echoes Heaney's phrasing but co-locates Hewitt's personal
sense of alienation alongside the older poet's Troubles-torn allusion:

And under each nipple

a deep incision, blade-width.

Even then, they needed boys
like me ...

This is an audacious writing of homosexuality into the world of Irish
poetry via its own deep and recent histories, but lightly done, as with
much else in this book. A similar deftness can be seen in Hewitt's translation of the Sweeney myth 'from *Buile Suibhne*', where locale and registers
share harmonic space with his own material. There are so many standout
poems in this collection that it's impossible to do it full justice here, but
the wonderful elegiac closing sequence, lamenting the loss of the poet's
father, showcases a beautifully felt simplicity which, nonetheless, carries
the weight of all big things. 'Tree of Jesse', in particular, had me gasping in
admiration at the way it manages to hold firm to its still wisdom, in those
unrepeatable days between a father's death and his burial; an intensely
personal liturgy of the hours in which living flesh transubstantiates into
time-torn idea:

and I felt in that moment
the privilege of being alive
in your mind, to have been remade

beyond myself and beamed out
in the flickering room of your sleep.
You are not leaving, I know,

but shifting into image – my head
already is haunted with you.
I have become a living afterlife.

Held within the lyric drift of this collection there are, too, moments of
equally brilliant nature writing in which Hewitt's search for the elemental
and sacred puts one in mind of those poets mentioned above:

It is here, by the swaying trees,
away from the glow of the house,

that I realise I have found myself at a place
so close to life, to its truth of violence ...
– 'KYRIE'

Against the backdrop of a young man attempting to make sense of his
father's demise ('what is a parent to a child but a god // who we turn to
when we still believe / that everything is fixable'), it is the unforced
simplicity of language that carries this collection's chief magic: that quality

of appearing to have always been widely felt but awaiting *this* expression. In his recent obituary for Derek Mahon, Sean O'Brien observed that his early collections 'were an inspiration and a challenge' to his contemporaries. I suspect Hewitt's debut might have a similar impact. I certainly hope so.

Since it generates an inscrutable energy entirely congruent with the severe landscape and routines of hard manual labour it depicts, Laurence O'Dwyer's *The Lighthouse Journal* is one of those collections that needs simply to be read and enjoyed rather than over-analysed. As per the title, there is a journalistic underpinning to the book's narrative arc, present most obviously in the prose poems that dominate its opening sequence, and register as an intriguing blend of Joseph Conrad with more recent aspects of nature and travel writing. O'Dwyer's pitch is attractive enough to draw the reader's initial interest: the book's narrator travels north through Europe, joining a distinctive cast of characters – Max, Julien, Elena, and a host of transient personalities – to spend the month between 'Wednesday April 27th' to 'Saturday May 27th' renovating the Litløy Fyr Lighthouse on its remote island overlooking the Lofoten archipelago in northern Norway. As someone who spent a month up at Sumburgh Head, I was bound to be hooked but there was far more than that to make this collection come alive for me. Firstly, I was impressed by the way in which O'Dwyer organises his material into a harmonious whole, in which the shifting floes of verse appear to drift naturally out of situation, timescale, personality, and recording. There are arcane histories, character studies, anthropology, and interesting new registers introduced to extend our expectations of what poetry might be, though never in a manner that seems forced. Each grows naturally out of a convincingly lived moment.

The protagonist of 'Maggot Time' reports –

> I woke last night in no-man's land; trudged downstairs to take a
> piss from the deck. Found everything furred in snow.

– while referencing the 'hybrid tongue' of *Russenorsk*. Its 'crude alloy of fish and scales and glue. Perfectly adaptable and blended like cheap whiskey' might, indeed, stand for the linguistic attributes of this collection. Also present is a discussion of masculinity amid the physical imperatives of living in extreme landscapes, often rendered with a hint of the mythic that I enjoyed, as in the blunt sign-off in 'Barbed Wire':

> I'm sure the gods hate him,
> but they can go fuck themselves.
> They volunteered to sit on their arse;
> he volunteered to work.

There's a lot of barbed wire in this book, as O'Dwyer conjures the sheer materiality of the place, both in terms of the work he did there and the distinctive nature of its landscape: 'The more the land / resembles a vanishing point, / the clearer our whereabouts become', he says in 'My First Norwegian Peak'. But it is those moments of Proustian unfolding that excite me most; in which the author draws upon his doctoral research to analyse the phenomenological bases of memory and poetically suggest how, wherever we are, we carry the whole world inside us:

> Eternally elsewhere, we rattle along the groove
> of the world, a needle drifting into the vinyl
> of the ocean, until we're lifted up
>
> and set down at the beginning of a memory,
> a song ...

—'SI PHAN DON'

Adam Crothers' second collection, *The Culture of My Stuff*, bounds up wagging its tail and frisky as a border collie, though this is not to underplay its serious achievement in getting us to ask interesting questions about the nature of language, rhythms, and registers. This is a Frankenstein's monster of a book stitched together from the disparate body parts of other texts, neologisms, and a clashing array of verbal, everyday, high-brow, and specialist registers. An early example of this might be 'Actaeon':

>   ... Your wig
> is unprofound: tip not that hat, straw man.
>
> Tip otherwise, and render void your till.
> Inscribe upon its vaults EMPTIED DAILY.
> *Id est*, love more. The polling stats suggest
>
> 'forgiveness' sounds divine.

The mental dexterity involved in this playfully heteroglossic approach is impressive, suggesting the verbal inventiveness of much early rap or Jamaican toasting, though this is not so much from the street as the Junior Common Room. It's reflected, too, in the fact that Crothers audaciously plunders – or seems to – every archaism or poetic *tick*-nique that comes to hand in order to form his threads; incorrigibly punning his way into your consciousness as he does so. And maybe mind-over-heart is the true domain of this collection. That's in no way an adverse judgment, rather a location of the book's core strength: it is altogether more arch than earnest, more punned against than sinning. Like a Ramones double Live album, however, *The Culture of My Stuff* maintains its ferociously inventive groove throughout, as in the long-lined 'Hammer Horror' from the collection's second section, 'Stuff':

> I'm all for one and a man for all seasons. Look like Percy Shelley, feel like Liam Neeson.
> *Cut like a buffalo?* the scriptures say; to oppose manifest destiny is high treason.

And even at the end Crothers finds the energy to slip in a spoof 'Notes and Acknowledgements' that cheekily posits –

> Earlier, some might say the earliest, versions of these poems were composed in the womb.

– before slipping in a couple more, one of which is the wry 'The Best Poem'. Some, indeed, might say that this 'joy bomb' tests the reader's patience at times of maximum pun, but I really liked its unremitting fun and enjoyed my tourette through the wired mind of a twenty-first century linguistic showman. Though, I do refer my honourable gentleman to the great Mark Eitzel's advice for showmen: sometimes, 'You gotta learn how to disappear in the silk and amphetamine.' On the evidence of this, I think he'd understand.

David Wheatley

ALL TO REPORT

Maurice Scully, *Things That Happen* (Shearsman Books, 2020), £19.95.

Though it may seem a period piece today, Donald Davie's *Thomas Hardy and British Poetry* (1972) is a compelling short study in (male) canons and canon formation. Still in recovery from his association with the Move-ment, Davie had invested heavily in Poundian modernist alternatives, and advocated energetically for the work of Ed Dorn and the Objectivists. When it came to British poetry, however, the argument snagged. Some-time in the post-Victorian age, British poetry had downsized, trading the human for the merely social. The representative British poet, from Hardy to Larkin, painted the social animal reconciling itself to necessity amid displays of touching pathos rather than anything more pyrotechnical ('Something is pushing them / To the side of their own lives'). And while Davie likes his Roy Fisher and JH Prynne – poets who don't follow this template – he doesn't quite know what to do with them, and either misreads them as defanged quietists, or the creatures of a disaffected fringe. Excitement and innovation were all very well if you were American, but were inherently un-British, unqualified to budge the British lyric from its moorings.

That was nearly fifty years ago, but Davie's is a critical pattern that has repeated itself prolifically across the intervening decades. I mention it here as a reminder of the ways in which poetry not written in the dominant style of its times will often end up condemned to a life of hos-tile onslaughts or nerdy fandom, casual airbrushing from the picture, or shunting into the bloodied margins. Irish poetry, too, has long enjoyed its own version of Davie's Thomas Hardy complex. Speaking to Dennis O'Driscoll, Seamus Heaney radiates a deep conviction that the avant-garde and its legacy are none of his concern ('It's an old-fashioned term by now. In literature, nobody can cause bother anymore'). True, Maurice Scully's name is often invoked by critics of the alternative persuasion, but when David Lloyd mentions him in the Cambridge UP series *Irish Literature in Transition* ('The Cultures of Poetry in Contemporary Ireland'), it is alongside Trevor Joyce and Catherine Walsh – fine poets both, but essentially the same team sheet that modernist-friendly critics have used for the last thirty years, with no younger names in sight. Is it Scully's fate to remain trapped in the crossfire of a decades-old culture war whose roots go all the way back to Beckett's 'Recent Irish Poetry' in 1934?

Let us hope not. The sheer scale of Scully's magnum opus, *Things That Happen*, means it carries its own historical dimension – begun in

1981, and completed twenty-five years later. Across its 600 pages and four sections (*5 Freedoms of Movement, Livelihood, Sonata*, and *Tig*), *Things That Happen* is a *roman fleuve* of consciousness on the move, a *Ducks, Newburyport* with added white space (and has a poet been keener on white space since Mallarmé? Between sequence titles, subtitles, and gnomic graphics, the longest section break I see here is effectively ten blank pages). One of Scully's jobs down the years has been nightwatchman, and in *The Basic Colours* he describes dutifully recording 'Site / normal. Nothing to report' in a logbook. *Things That Happen* is forever scanning the field of consciousness, on the lookout for the small daily ripples in the flow, and crossing like a tightrope the connecting thread whereby 'one thing leads to another'.

In one of the sequence's found-text moments, Scully recycles an unwelcome financial warning informing him that 'you are continuing to avail / yourself of unauthorised credit'. As Scully strikes out into unfamiliar territory, he gives the impression of turning that 'unauthorised credit' into a *modus operandi*, following its leads without much regard for the usual desire paths of Irish writing. Or rather, he re-lays those paths for his own ends, as in his repeated returns to Seán Ó Ríordáin's 'Saoirse' ('Raghaidh mé síos i measc na ndaoine'), but very much an Ó Ríordáin as you will not have heard him before ('I'll go down: tonight. Yes. / Tiny animate creatures connect. Proliferate. / This house; that star. Bless'). One area where comparisons do suggest themselves freely is painting. Writing on him previously, I have compared Scully to Paul Klee, that most ludic of artists. While that still holds good, I would now throw Matisse into the mix as well, given how Klee tended to work on a miniature scale and how adept Matisse and Scully are at splashing primary colours about in large-scale gestures. Even down to the *sprezzatura* of his oversized (often two-page) 'Sonnets', the maximalism is carefree-euphoric, not overweening-ponderous.

5 Freedoms of Movement features some detailed descriptions of a semi-demolished house, and the interpenetration of inside and outside, completeness and the fragmentary seem very congenial to Scully, in a kind of erotics of ruins:

> being a porous membrane
> tra-la world moving through
> it as if mist made of mist gone
> to Standa Maurice back soon
> as allwhen through ambitact
>
> to make a bedframe creak
> for a little while

in the half-light
giving your nerve-ends a good time.
flower   table   stem

Scully talks of 'ambitact' here, and elsewhere of the 'delicious tact of / of things intact', which even when handled retain their sense of generous surprise. The flea-like hop, skips and jumps hang in the air like a Calder mobile, to use a comparison employed in interview by Scully himself; poetry is 'an activity not a body of reading', and learning to keep up with Scully's *prestissimo* pace is all part of the training. 'Only emotion endures', wrote Pound, to which Scully, or an interlocutor of his in *The Basic Colours*, replies 'but how can you write about emotion / when you forget everything the next day?' Scully's poetry is as full of emotion and lyric colour as anyone could want, but you'll have to tie them down pretty fast to stop them getting away.

I can't do more than suggest a flavour of Scully's work in a short review like this, and therefore feel all the guiltier for embarking on digressions about canons and canonicity. But how we read poetry today is less than ideally suited to Scully, whose works needs to be absorbed *in extenso*, not in the bite-sized anthology slots (or Instagram posts?) by which short lyric poems embed themselves in public consciousness. Perhaps the essays collected in Kenneth Keating's edited collection, *A Line of Tiny Zeros in the Fabric: Essays on the Poetry of Maurice Scully* (Shearsman Books, 2020), will help to create a proper context for reading him. Unfortunately, I haven't seen it yet so can't comment, though no sooner did I finish *Things That Happen* than I received a recent 200-page book of Scully's, *Play Book* (Coracle, 2019), which I look forward to reading. 'The thing about poetry is', we read in *Adherence*, in a proposition that Scully archly chooses not to complete. The thing about Scully is that no com-pleted version of that sentence (including this sentence) does justice to the full experience of reading this most inconclusive and playful of modern Irish poets. Long may the last word be lacking.

Catherine Gander

TOPOGRAPHIES OF DISPLACEMENT

Natalie Diaz, *Postcolonial Love Poem* (Faber & Faber, 2020), £10.99.
Bhanu Kapil, *How to Wash a Heart* (Liverpool University Press, 2020), £9.99.

Natalie Diaz's second collection, *Postcolonial Love Poem*, a finalist for the
Forward Prize and the National Book Award, is one of the most important collections to come out of America in recent years. Latinx and ʻAha
Makav (in Spanish, Mojave), and an enrolled member of the Gila River
Indian tribe, Diaz well understands the inadequacy of the term 'postcolonial' and of the language of the oppressor to communicate the conditions
of living and loving in the wake of imperial violence. Countering the
linear, white-skewed interpretation of history that the word 'postcolonial'
tends to encourage, Diaz's extraordinary book weaves languages and
cultures, communal and personal stories, lyric verse and prose poem,
to craft a poetics that decentres the patriarchal, colonial gaze and fore-
grounds brown, queer, nonbinary perspectives.

   Diaz's 'love poem' is written for the various bodies and souls that
colonialism's ongoing history still seeks to erase – *'our many bodies of flesh,
language, land, and water'*, she writes in the book's dedication, *'the missing
and murdered Indigenous and Native women, girls, trans women, nonbinary
and two spirit people in our families, communities, and across the Americas and
other occupied lands'*. Such corpora populate Diaz's book, whose lines
wind through the labyrinthine entanglements of oppression and resistance, occupation and displacement, geology and mythology, love and
war, tenderness and pain. These conditions are charted across the twin
topographies of the earth and the human body, which Diaz tells us in
her exquisite poem, 'The First Water is the Body', are forever linked 'in
Mojave thinking':

> The words are separated only by the letters ʻii and ʻa: ʻiimat for body,
> ʻamat for land. In conversation, we often use a shortened form for
> each: *mat-*. Unless you know the context of a conversation, you might
> not know if we are speaking about our body or our land. You might
> not know which has been injured, which is remembering, which is
> alive, which was dreamed, which needs care. You might not know
> we mean both.

Knowing the context is one thing; speaking the language is another.
Removed from close communion with the earth, non-Native Americans
lack a key component to its comprehension. The colonial project to

occupy land continues to cost lives. The earth's life sources continue to be polluted by capitalist enterprise (think of the Dakota pipeline, or the effects of climate change). 'If I say, *My river is disappearing*, do I also mean, *My people are disappearing?*', Diaz asks. 'How can I translate—not in words but in belief—that a river is a body, as alive as you or I, that there can be no life without it?'

The answer, for Diaz, in part resides in a return to the primordial quality of the earth's essential elements. The rise and fall of her chest, the dips and contours of her lover's hips, the flux and flow of the Colorado River, contain a kind of pre-verbal poetry, brimming with 'being, energy, prayer, current, motion, medicine' ('The First Water Is the Body'). Movement is key: after all, there is no such thing as still life. This healing energy undulates across the book, surfacing in the collection's poems of sensual, sexual union. Here, Diaz's poetry reaches into a realm where the sonic quality of words translates a sensorial, embodied transcendence; logic falls away to felt knowledge and cultural memory. In 'Skin-Light', Diaz blends, in sensuous, breath-stopped, stepped lines, two ancient rituals of love-making and play in the twists of light between dark bodies:

> I put my mouth there—: mercy-luxed, and come, we both,

> to light. It streams me.
> A rush of scorpions—:
>   fast-light. A lash of breath—:
>   god-maker.

> Light horizons her hip—: springs an ocelot
> cut of chalcedony and magnetite.
>   Hip, limestone and cliffed,

> slopes like light into her thigh—: light-box, skin-bound.

Despite the freedom and release that sex and writing bring, however, the coloniser continues to invade the most private, intimate moments of both. In 'Manhattan Is a Lenape Word', images of sex, loneliness, wildness, and war all haunt the poet's stay in a New York hotel, where she is the 'only Native American / on the 8th floor'. As her mind shuttles from the city's hive-like colonisation of the sky to her lover's body, dark and sweet as honey, a language of love emerges that bears a sting: '*She is mine, colony.*' One can occupy a body (one's own, another's), or a country (one's own, another's) with love, or with force, and Diaz reminds us of the violence lurking in a particularly American expression of ownership:

She says, *You make me feel*
like lightning. I say, *I don't ever*
want to make you feel that white.
It's too late—I can't stop seeing
her bones. I'm counting the carpals,
metacarpals of her hand inside me.

[...]

Somewhere far from New York City,
an American drone finds then loves
a body—the radiant nectar it seeks
through great darkness—makes
a candle-hour of it, and burns
gently along it, like American touch,
an unbearable heat.

Diaz's language often slips between love and destruction, between
identities and bodies, as easily as a tongue or a river – both recurrent
images in her book. There's a deep, sensuous liquidity to her writing that
absorbs and transports us: to read it is a somatic experience.

In 'That Which Cannot Be Stilled', one of the poems that arose from
her correspondence with the poet Ada Limón, Diaz considers the
identities that have been imprinted upon her, including 'Dirty Indian—a
phrase blown like magnetite dust / against the small bones of my ear'.
How to rid oneself of a slur that sticks, a corruption of language, an
untruth? 'All my life I've been working, / to get clean', Diaz writes, 'to be
clean is to be good, in America.' Yet the water that runs through the
collection does not exist to purify, but to move across planes, to bring
life. 'If we poison and use up our water', Diaz asks, 'how will we wash
away what we must leave behind us? How will we make ourselves new?'
Her book is a love letter and invocation to love, not passively, not hum-
bly, but with the force and self-generating newness of a river – of poetry.
This kind of love resists colonial erasure. 'Let me tell you a story about
water', concludes '*exhibits from* The American Water Museum',

Once upon a time there was us.
America's thirst tried to drink us all away.
And here we still are.

When Bhanu Kapil wrote to the poet and interventional cardiologist,
Ankur Kalra, for information about his work, he spoke of the realities of
'broken heart syndrome', of how 'anxiety and shock have an effect' on
'the immigrant heart'. His diagnosis pulses through the pages of Kapil's

slim new volume, which grew out of her performance art piece at the ICA in 2019, and is her first full-length collection to be published in the UK. Written in the voice of an immigrant guest in the home of a citizen host, *How To Wash A Heart* explores the disintegrating relationship between guest and host, revealing the ways the rooms of a guesthouse, like the chambers of the human heart, can rapidly become inhospitable to life.

Free verse, yet stacked on the left of the page like small book towers, or bodies pressed against a wall, Kapil's poems communicate a mounting sense of being edged out of existence. Toward the start of the book, her lines are longer, yet contain the conditions of adjustment and gratitude required of the newly transplanted immigrant:

> You made a space for me in your home, for my books and clothes, and I'll
> Never forget that.
> When your adopted daughter, an "Asian refugee"
> As you described her,
> Came in with her coffee and perched on the end
> Of my cot, I felt so happy.
> And less like a hoax.

As the speaker's narrative unfolds, her lines dip into memory and loop back into her present as she attempts to reconcile the embodied experiences of both. When her host asks her to describe her 'long journey', the response is met with disappointment. Images of beauty and happiness are undesirable: 'No, you said / I want to hear what happened afterwards / Not before.' The colonial appetite for trauma tourism that is woven into what Teju Cole has famously called 'the white-saviour industrial complex' taints an already strained relationship:

> The host-guest chemistry
> Is inclusive, complex, molecular,
> Dainty.
> Google it.

The imperative to self-educate is directed at the reader as much as to the host: two sides of the same coin. For this reason, the use of the second person pronoun 'you' throughout the poems extends an address that slides between intimacy and exclusion, complicity and accusation. What questions arise from this dynamic? What forms does acceptance take – or hospitality, or love? What does the reader want, or expect, from the art they are holding in their hand, or placing on their living-room bookshelf? There's something performative and vampiric about the aesthetic of care the white, middle-class host seeks to create in their 'desire for art / That comes from a foreign / Place'. And while, like Kapil herself, the poems' speaker makes art out of her predicament, it's an art, to repurpose Elizabeth Bishop's words, of losing:

> The art of crisis
> Is that you no longer
> Think of home
> As a place for social respite.
> Instead, it's a ledge
> Above a narrow canyon.
>
> [...]
>
> How do you live when the link
> Between creativity
> And survival
> Can't easily
> Be discerned?

As Kapil writes in one of the first poems of the book: 'It's exhausting to be a guest / In somebody else's house / Forever.' The effect / affect is similar to living under occupation, or a regime; one must abide by rules spoken and unspoken, one must learn to read the dangers that crouch in silences as well as reside in words: 'Is silence an axe / Raised above the head?' Under the waning light of the welcome sign, the immigrant guest is both exoticised and erased in a type of colonial cleansing; the speaker wonders at the intention behind her host's quiet gift of a vaginal douche and medicated powder.

As anti-immigrant rhetoric increases in Europe and the US, Kapil's poems ask us, in searing, embodied language, to examine the slippage between ritual and charade, 'When what you perform / At the threshold / Is at odds / With what happens / When the front door is closed.'

In this remarkable series of poems containing images both precise and enveloping, Kapil builds a discomfiting, destabilising tension, and as the speaker's story moves toward its devastating climax, the book poses more questions than it suggests answers. How to wash a heart? 'Remove it then pack it / In ice'. The method entails displacement from context, the creation of a cavity, a ritualistic practice of removal in which so much stands to be lost.

Julie Morrissy

COVENANT

Doireann Ní Ghríofa, *A Ghost in the Throat* (Tramp Press, 2020), €16.

A Ghost in the Throat openly invites readers into the complexities of the lives of women in Ireland – and insists on our importance. Despite its very recent publication, Doireann Ní Ghríofa's prose debut has already been heralded as a significant contribution to Irish non-fiction. Her status as a celebrated and bilingual Irish poet is well-known and, given her expansive practice, this most recent step into prose should not come as a surprise. Ní Ghríofa's ability to get inside different modes of expression is notable in *A Ghost in the Throat*. The book brings the reader on a quest narrative of sorts, in which one poet becomes consumed with the life of another, Eibhlín Dubh Ní Chonaill. We follow Ní Ghríofa as she follows Ní Chonaill, an eighteenth-century poet and author of 'Caoineadh Airt Uí Laoghaire', a lament written on the occasion of her husband's death. The book's momentum is wrapped up in Ní Ghríofa's self-declared obsession with the poem, which she first encounters as a schoolgirl. It returns to her as a teenager and then later as an adult when she passes a sign for Kilcrea while moving house with her family. The location becomes stuck in her head until she finally remembers that Kilcrea is the burial place of Art Ó Laoghaire. I found myself nodding along with the challenges the writer faces, from moving on the whim of landlords to familiar 'constellations of black mould'. The mould is mentioned only in passing, but the image lingers as Ní Ghríofa's fixation also slowly grips and grows.

Throughout the book, she refers to her subject simply as Eibhlín Dubh, reinforcing the closeness and familiarity she feels as an Irish speaker towards the poet. When reflecting on her young response to the 'Caoineadh', Ní Ghríofa recalls her teenage description of the poem: 'She jumps on his horse and rides away with him forever.' The rapid manner and energy of Ní Ghríofa's investigation is reminiscent of a horse bolting. As she becomes increasingly enthralled, the author's daily focus remains fixed on this historic poem and on the poet's life. In addition to Ní Ghríofa's own translation of the 'Caoineadh', the book also weaves together two stories: one about Ní Ghríofa, and the other about Eibhlín Dubh.

Ní Ghríofa thoroughly and thoughtfully recounts the details of Eibhlín Dubh's life, as well as the lengths of her efforts and research in uncovering those facts. The reader enjoys a meaningful look into the life of the poet, her relationship with her husband Art, and the wider context and circumstances of Eibhlín Dubh's existence. The book describes

Ní Ghríofa's escapades, 'stealing into libraries', copying documents to add to her notes, in an endless quest to find out more about her subject. This diligent and meticulous nature is further reflected in other areas, including her involvement in 'the milk bank' through which Ní Ghríofa donates her own breast milk for premature babies: 'I check the readout from my freezer thermometer and note the digits carefully, initial my chart, then settle the newly cooled bottle alongside eight identical bricks in the freezer, the yield of a good week. At a certain time every morning, my kitchen resembles a lab ...'. Her fastidious nature encompasses all her ventures and, as the books unfolds, we witness the author's dogged mission to illuminate Eibhlín Dubh's life. That journey is rife with set-backs and dead ends, as it becomes clear that Ní Chonaill's life has not been documented or honoured in Ireland's deep and rich poetry tradition. One chapter describes the process through which poems were historically commissioned by *taoisigh* and then written by male bards: 'The poems were then copied into *duanairí*, handwritten anthologies that often also held genealogies and sacred texts. By contrast, literature composed by women was not stored in books but in female bodies, living repositories of poetry and song.' These questions about gender and the erasure of women continue to arise as Ní Ghríofa delves further into her subject, and, sadly, these issues are not unfamiliar to Irish women writers, even in very recent times.

One thing I find enchanting is Ní Ghríofa's wholehearted embracing of her imaginary worlds, and not only in regard to her interest in Eibhlín Dubh. When discussing the milk bank, she mentions karma and her 'sympathy for the imagined babies and their imagined families'. However, another strong and complementary element arises from Ní Ghríofa's self-awareness and sometimes even self-critique. She balances her imagination with a forthright nature, admitting that perhaps her volunteer activities also provide the 'illusion of control'. There is ample strong, feminist work being written in this book but, for me, one of the most striking elements is how candidly Ní Ghríofa writes about herself and her own motiva-tions. What she reveals is refreshing and, at times, a little sad because of the ways in which she talks about domestic work in particular. Early in the book, she says, 'I sweep. I wash. I tidy. I am one of The Many whose working day does not have a clocking-out time ... There is a peculiar contentment to be found in absenting oneself like this, subsumed in the needs of others: in such erasure, for me, lies joy.' The honesty of these lines makes me think about how deeply embedded those habits of eras-ure can become, reinforcing the importance of a book like *A Ghost in the Throat*.

Later, when the author is searching for the flour mill where Eibhlín Dubh mourned, she writes, 'I have exhausted myself lately, absenting myself from my own days to seek the days of another, and I have begun to feel troubled by my behaviour, questioning whether my attempts are really any more useful than the abrupt lines of biography that first provoked me ... I walk the length of the village again, trying and trying to find some remnant of that structure. Again, I fail. I fail her, I fail you, and I fail myself.' In these lines, Ní Ghríofa reaches out to her reader, confronting and inviting us into all the complexities and difficulties of her voyage into Eibhlín Dubh Ní Chonaill's life, but also her own journey, as she navigates through life.

Owing to Ní Ghríofa's insistent cataloguing and detailing of her life and that of Eibhlín Dubh's, I am reminded of other books relating to the lives of Irish women writers. Naturally, I think often about Eavan Boland's *Object Lessons*, especially the lines, 'it was possible to be a poet, permissible to be a woman and difficult to be both without flouting the damaged and incomplete permissions on which Irish poetry had been constructed.' Ní Ghríofa sharply underlines Boland's critique, made from a different generation but one that resurfaces in *A Ghost in the Throat*. We are reminded that the permissions are still incomplete, and not solely in terms of gender.

I start to think more about the manner in which Irish women writers are written about, and my mind turns to Terese Svoboda's biography of Lola Ridge, *Anything That Burns You*. Again, that book represents one poet writing the life of another, dedicating time, space, and attention to an Irish woman on the page. In *The Midnight*, Susan Howe too ventures into the life of an Irish woman writer, her mother Mary Manning. I recall a passage titled 'Irish Literary Revival' in which Howe reveals that her mother would always carry a book by Matthew Arnold with her and, in one instance, carried it through 'the Brontë moors in Yorkshire'. Howe continues, 'I am to read aloud the last three paragraphs of *Wuthering Heights* for the sixth grade public reading contest ... The book is [my mother's] choice. Poetry is our covenant.'

Ní Ghríofa stuffs photocopies about Eibhlín Dubh under her bed, flinging a tattered copy of the 'Caoineadh' into her hospital bag as she urgently rushes to the maternity ward owing to complications in her pregnancy. Poetry, too, is her covenant, though she describes herself as 'merely a woman who loves this poem'. And yet, in her decision to follow her passion for poetry and poets, Ní Ghríofa contributes something powerful – not just to Irish writing but to Irish life.

AN INTERVIEW WITH PAULA MEEHAN

Adam Wyeth talks to **Paula Meehan**, on the occasion of the publication of her *As If By Magic: Selected Poems* (Dedalus Press).

Adam Wyeth: Can you say something about the title, *As If By Magic*, and some of the symbolism around it?

Paula Meehan: It's a phrase in the demotic that I've always liked. I would have heard it nearly every day from my granny. "As if by magic, your father put the rent together." Or, "As if by magic they had the last three chops down in the butchers." Often, you'd hear it attached to a stroke of luck, or it presaged some rigmarole with a happy or curious ending. The title also bounces off a poem of mine, 'Well' – I was going to use a line from that, 'I know this path by magic', or 'the magic path'. Magic has been foundational to the way I practise and make poetry. The idea that poetry is a kind of magic, that it is even sacred at certain times, is something that's prevalent in all cultures, I think. We can trace poetry back to early magical and ritualistic uses of language to draw animals to the hunters, to appease unseen forces, to change consciousness. I'm also very interested in medicine bundles, collections of things that are put together, and that have a healing, medicinal power. I just make power objects from language.

AW: That poem, 'Well', which you mentioned, has become your signature poem over the years. You often begin readings with it. Can you talk to me about how this poem came to be written?

PM: I was living very remote for a few years in Co. Leitrim. 'Well' was part of a sequence of ten poems that were inspired from a Celtic Cross spread from *The Elemental Tarot*, which I've used since the 1980s when it was published. I used the cards as focuses for meditation and then just wrote the poems straight out of what the cards were suggesting. But the poem 'Well' and the sequence also came out of my day-to-day life in the Leitrim landscape, becoming more aware of natural cycles. There had been a fire in the utility plant that treated our water supply. Soldiers were on the street warning us not to drink the water from our taps because it was coming untreated straight from the Shannon. We were living relatively near the river's source. So a lot of people were cleaning out their own old local wells to get good water. This idea that this magnificent river, which runs like an artery right through the centre of Ireland, was unsafe even that close to its source, really hit me. This idea of sources vulnerable to corruption fed into a lot of the work I did subsequently.

AW: *As If By Magic* selects work from over three decades. How did you go about compiling these poems? Was it a very fraught process, deciding what to choose and what to exclude, or did you have a clear idea in your mind?

PM: I found the process very strange, almost like a kind of regression therapy, revisiting the emotions and times of my life when the poems were made. I didn't realise how much I had written out of trauma, both in my private life and in the life of the communities I lived and worked in. The book started out as a Collected Poems. My initial idea was to gather everything together from all the disparate sources published and unpublished and have it ready for my sixty-fifth birthday in June of 2020. But I decided not to republish my first two collections and concentrate on a generous Selected; it has the guts of my last five books. When I came out the other side, I felt an enormous amount of gratitude that life had dealt me a hand I was allowed to play through these poems. Poetry has been a protective path for me to be on. I could have taken many other paths that mightn't have been so protective of the self and psyche.

AW: Going back to those early days of the Eighties, can you describe the atmosphere of Dublin back then and your way into the poetry scene?

PM: I had started making poems in my teens, in the Seventies, which was a fantastically vital time for music, especially for lyrics. Dylan! Mitchell! Cohen! Wonderful models, and I would have aspired then to making songs. I was very into dance and drama, into painting and Buddhism, especially through the conduit of American poetry, though I wouldn't have been into gurus and any hierarchical stuff, having watched what unquestioned authority did to the Catholic Church I was raised in. It was exciting to be a teenager in Finglas then, and I had a great gang of pals. Street theatre would have been one of the first places where I really felt the power of language and the possibilities of what language could do: transmitting ideas through ritualized language. I started publishing in the Eighties after years of travelling and a Master of Fine Arts degree in the USA. I arrived home to the great Eighties recession, to butter vouchers and the dole and the free-range life of the poet. Gradually, I put a net of survival together. Workshops in the prisons, in communities where I'd grown up, the inner city, in Finglas, and in Fatima Mansions where I lived then, a community in crisis. Everywhere sustained by the amazing spirit of the people I was connecting to in the communities and in the arts. Then there were the years in Leitrim, where I really settled into intense poetry making, heart, mind, and soul.

AW: How was it navigating the poetry world of Dublin and working out of an Irish tradition which is so male-dominated in poetry? Was it a challenge to break through the historical monoliths like Yeats, for example?

PM: One of the early poems that I didn't include in this Selected is called 'The Apprentice', and it's a reckoning with Yeats. In the poem I say, 'I walked on new laid roads conjuring a hazel wood'; 'My women must be hollow of cheek with poverty and the whippings of history'; 'You are no master of mine, who gilds the heart and blinds the eye.' It was about my own need to break through the literary legacy to my own space. I was literally walking on new-laid roads of concrete in the new estate. When I first met Eavan Boland, who became a friend, I felt I had to ask her a really grown-up poetry question. I was talking about Yeats and asking how do you get out from under his shadow? She said I could try writing in his light. That was a moment of realisation for me – that I could turn my argument into some kind of power that I could use in my work. I have to say I am a dyed-in-the-wool feminist. I was lucky enough to be born into a family of powerful women. And I was lucky too that I had a protective arrogance when I was starting out – fuelled by an anti-authoritarian streak. So I didn't wait around for permission. I'd still be waiting.

AW: I like that idea of making something out of those oppressive energies. I often think of literature as one long conversation that writers have with those who have gone before us.

PM: We work with inherited materials; the language and every single word comes with its ghosts. On a practical level, one of the ways of recognising a good line of poetry, for me, is that the ghosts of the words are harmonising. Their etymologies feed into the power of the line. I adored the Romantics when I was a young woman. Shelley, 'I fall upon the thorns of life. I bleed.' That was me. In a way you are hostage to what the education system offers you as 'tradition': as you get older and have a wider set of cultural references, and you see who has power and why, you start to elect your own tradition, to find the sustenance you need, I believe, and to question what you are being offered as the canon and who is proposing it and why. Essentially, you begin to discern the politics of the arts world, the poetry world, and you see through the individuals who are power-mongering. And you learn to make your own path and crucially to avoid becoming a victim of other people's agendas. Most important lessons are learned the hard way, in poetry as in life. The poetry scene can be toxic and people can get hurt. I often think poets should be putting on Samurai armour, enamelled deerskin to deflect the blades of swords. The safest place to take yourself is into the work, to channel your energy into the work. That brings me back to the power of the thing itself. The native/indigenous cultures usually understand power objects. Where something is made with open heart, with ferocious love – and with always the ambition to grow as a craftswoman, to advance as an artist – it is my experience that the poems themselves draw to you what you need to survive.

AW: Do you have an example of a standout 'power object' poem from the Selected, where you were able to transform this energy into a poem?

PM: The poem 'Home'. It goes back to 1994 – and it goes back to Ciaran Carson, another great pal who's gone the road beyond. Ciaran sent me off on tour in the North when he was literature and traditional music officer of the Northern Ireland Arts Council. It was just before the first ceasefire, which didn't hold, but was a stepping-stone to the peace process. Off I went, with – amongst other traditional musicians – a fantastic fiddler in his eighties, Big John McManus from Aughakillymaude, Derrylin, in South Fermanagh, and his wife, Valerie, who had a lovely hoard of songs (we called her Diamond Lil in cognizance of her days in the showbands), and Cathal McConnell, lord of misrule, who played the flute and other instruments. We'd travel in a little van around the North in that dark time of random sectarian violence – there were paramilitaries dressing up in the uniform of the regular army or the garb of the other side, stopping cars and just shooting people. It was wild stuff. Our tour took us into pubs, theatres, community centres, I'd never be quite sure who the audience was. Once I opened my mouth and read a poem such as 'My Father Perceived as a Vision of St Francis', you could sense the nods: 'Catholic, Catholic, Catholic.' You realise how much poetry hangs out your cultural baggage. Whereas the music could jump the sectarian divide – well, many tunes and songs might. It was a fascinating trip and I loved every terrifying minute of it. Big John McManus had hung up his fiddle for a long time, now he was taking it back down for the tour and coming on the road as an old man. Early on he was working at remembering tunes, and you could nearly hear the rusty cogs of his memory turning. By the end of the tour, over the few weeks we travelled together, the tradition was flowing through him. He was its instrument. That showed me something about my relationship with tradition – that I could open up channels and let it flow through me. 'Home', the poem that came out of that tour, embodied the power I experienced from direct transmission.

AW: It sounds like this was a bit of a Joycean epiphany for you. Have you had many significant epiphanic moments, where your writing life opened up in a new way or took you in a new direction?

PM: In Yeats's small perfect play *The Cat and the Moon*, a blind beggar and a lame beggar are searching for the holy well of St Colman. When they get to the holy well, St Colman manifests himself and offers them a choice of being cured or being blessed. So my epiphany happened back in the Seventies when I was a member of a street theatre troupe. We were working with groups of children from the inner city, performing *The Cat and the Moon* on Dollymount Strand among the dunes.

One particular morning, whatever was in the air, by the time we guided the children to the rim of the dune and the saint made his appearance, the children fell to their knees, their hands joined as if at church. Suddenly a boy of about eight or nine years of age got up off his knees and walked down the slope of the dune until he was standing right in front of the saint. His hands were still joined and he spoke reverently to our actor: "Holy St Colman, will you cure me please? Will you give me back me boy's voice?" He had a beautiful melodious Dublin voice, but there were no two ways about it – if you'd had your eyes closed you would be sure it was a girl had spoken. It was such a huge outpouring of sorrow from such a small frame. We were stunned. At a total loss. For one moment it felt as if the actor playing the saint *could* utter a cure and give him back his boy's voice. The moment passed. The actor spoke, as gently and kindly as he could, about how we each have an individual voice that is important and unique. But, there was no miracle. From that day on we were careful to let the children see us making up and getting into character. We wanted a willing suspension of disbelief. We also wanted an informed suspension of disbelief. We didn't want to mess with their hearts and minds.

AW: Many of your best-loved poems are in this book. Can you tell me how 'My Father Perceived as a Vision of St Francis' came to be written?

PM: 'My Father Perceived as a Vision of St Francis' was a breakthrough moment. I remember writing it when I was Writer Fellow in Residence in Trinity College Dublin back in the day. There I was in these beautiful old rooms where Brendan Kennelly had written his masterpiece, *Cromwell*, one of the great liberating poems of our tradition. This poem just came out of the blue, about my father, and I understood it was about a tender maleness, a nurturing male figure, which is something I would have been interested in as a feminist – puzzling out what the male tradition might offer. I was very conscious that I would have got poetry very much through the male line. So that poem came out in a surge of gratitude, for Brendan to whom it's dedicated, and for the kind of roots and pathways that were opened to me even by poetry that I had an argument with. Because sometimes the argument is the driving force.

AW: As well as studying at Trinity College Dublin, you did your MFA at Eastern Washington University. You studied with many fine poets, such as Gary Snyder. Can you say something about this experience?

PM: I feel especially grateful for the teachers I've had both inside and outside the academy. One of the most important workshops I ever attended was with Gary Snyder back in 1982-83. The first workshop he gave was all about breath. I had asked him, "What do you do about fear?" He taught us one breath meditation; bringing all your consciousness to the one breath. And of course, one breath is all you need for a line. That sounds terribly strange and simple, but it was so profound to me and doable. If you can manage that one breath you'll probably manage the next one.

AW: Do you still suffer from nerves before a reading?

PM: Yes, it's awful, but I have techniques to help. At the same time I really believe in direct transmission with poetry, a direct transmission that might even circumvent language itself. So it's not just *what* the poem is about, but *how* the poem is about what it's about. That's what directly goes into you at a reading – and that is magic.

AW: How else did the academic life influence your work? Did you find the workshop approach from America to be very inspiring?

PM: I think most poets start off in an expressive mode. But my great teacher James J McAuley, who taught me prosody at Washington State, put my work under a huge amount of pressure. It was a workshop system with a lot of form and theory. He dared me to take on the received forms, the patterns handed down through time. I adored the song forms, I made many early attempts at sonnets and especially villanelles, which came into the English tradition from the troubadours.

AW: Dennis O'Driscoll believed poets have a particular word that is specific to them. If you did have one such word, what do you think it might be?

PM: 'Light'. That's all I want really, light and all it transfigures. I imagine I could actually live on light. I think in these times, you've to work a bit harder to embrace light, to go towards the light. Even within our own selves, to move through the things that are most difficult, the shadows. I'm always trying to push towards a place of light rather than be overwhelmed by the darkness of it. Every time you bring to full consciousness some unconscious or subconscious material it feels like there's more yet to come, that the work is never done. Those elements often emerge through dream.

AW: Are dreams an important source for your creative life?

PM: I would use dreams a great deal. I am directed by dreams. I think they are eruptions from something going on far back there, and they're telling me a story. I think a dream and a poem are very close. I've done a lot of dreamwork over the years, including a system called Projective Dreamwork with a great friend of mine, Juliet Clancy. It's a communal process based on Jeremy Taylor's work. You offer your dream (the way in a workshop you'd offer your poem), to be heard by the group, and each person has a chance to say what they think of it *as if it were their own dream*. Each person then constructs a narrative. It would bring different associations or memories to the fore. The person whose dream it is just sits and listens. The process is based on an assumption that we dream not only for ourselves but for each other, and we dream for our communities.

AW: That's really interesting, to see how a dream can be workshopped in the same way as a poem, and also then turned into poetry. The more I read Jung's theories around the unconscious and dreamwork, the more I see how interconnected it is to literature and creativity. I guess if the poem and dream emerge from the unconscious, there's little difference?

PM: Well, the poem is made in language, the dream may be pre-language, or may attain language to be transmitted. I love the dreamscapes. I think that poetry too can have that kind of function in a community, that we carry poems for each other and for our communities. I've always thought that poetry is the history of the dreaming of the human race.

AW: French painter and critic Jean Bazaine said, 'Nobody paints as he likes. All a painter can do is to will with all his might the painting his age is capable of.' Are you aware of working within a kind of zeitgeist?

PM: I was very influenced by Gary Snyder, by his great radical vision – his essays from the Fifties, Sixties, Seventies are still radical today. Up the mountain he asks, "Is there a senator for all this?" What is our responsibility as poets for the earth and our fellow creatures? Is there an injunction to speak for the non-human? What can the poet speak for in this time when the human species itself has been capable of biocide on the natural world? So I did take that idea of who speaks for the mountain, who speaks for the wolf, who speaks for the bear, who speaks for the coastal meadow, the stand of pines? There's been an attempt to side-line work like this into a ghetto called 'eco-poetry'. The issues are too vital for it to go into a ghetto. The destruction of creation, our beautiful home, is a mainstream concern now. It's interesting how the fringes in poetry tend to shift into the mainstream. I think there is something in the dreaming self that can see what's coming up the trail. If you write that it's called prophecy.

AW: Do you think poetry still has a strong part to play in the world?

PM: All I know is, if it wasn't useful, if we didn't need it in each generation that keeps producing poets, those ritualists of language, poetry would have died off. Evolution is relentless and it doesn't do anyone any favours. If it's not useful it withers away. There's no sign of poetry disappearing.

AW: Do you feel like you have responsibilities as an artist, either to an audience or to yourself?

PM: Sometimes I've had to say things that might not be palatable to people I love. I think the only responsibility is to truth, and to your own truth, and to transmit your own truth. My responsibility as both a human and a poet answers to *Ahimsa*, a Buddhist precept. Non-violence, or at least, doing least harm, because being part of the food chain involves something dying so we may live. 'We live on the dead and the down', as Snyder puts it. Eavan Boland has it in her marvellous poem, for me the most political poem of our time, 'Making Money'. Boland writes about those turn of the century mill girls making the high quality paper that was exported all over Europe, paper the currencies of empire was printed on, paper made in mills powered by the rivers that came down through Dundrum running towards the Liffey. (*Slang* is the name of one of the little rivers, which I think is a wonderful linguistic flourish.) They literally made money, but not for themselves. In the poem Boland writes, 'the past is a crime'. It's a powerful utterance.

AW: I read that Elizabeth Bishop took twenty years to complete her great poem, 'The Moose'. Does it take you years sometimes to complete poems?

PM: I have notebooks that go back forty years. I have a strong relation-ship with these notebooks. I see them as compost heaps. The poem I wrote for Seamus Heaney, to mark his seventieth birthday, had a long gestation period, before it became the sonnet, 'A Remembrance of my Grandfather, Wattie, Who Taught Me to Read and Write'. I wanted to make a toy for Seamus, something playful, wrought, that he would get a bit of craic out of. Also, I wanted to talk about the male line of inheritance. My grandfather taught me to read and write before I went to school. He gave me that most important tool which I've been using ever since. So when I went into the primary school system as a girl from the tenements I could use that tool to decode to a certain degree what was endangering me. There was a lot of trying to keep safe in dangerous situations. I wanted to tie in this idea of my grandfather's gift of writing and of course Seamus's gift to our spirits of his extraordinary works. Ten years or so before I wrote the poem, I was walking through Merrion Square and there was an old book way up high in an oak tree and I jotted a note, 'What the #$%@ is that book doing up in the tree?' I found the note while riffling through the notebooks and that turned into the poem for Seamus. But if I hadn't made that note all those years before, I wouldn't have had the poem. That's the lovely looping of the work, things don't have to be made in the moment. But the attention and the recording of the attention can feed later work. The notebooks become a huge resource.

AW: Do you get many poems which come out complete in the first draft?

PM: There are a few poems like that in the book. I long for them, but I don't get very many. 'Lullaby' I wrote for my younger sister when she was pregnant, that came out complete. I had the tune of the traditional lullaby in my ear. Sometimes I'm conscious I'm writing to a tune, an old tune. 'My Father Perceived as a Vision of St Francis' came out pretty much as it is, just needed a little bit of fine-tuning. The ones that are heavily worked and wrought, they may be okay, I accept them, but they wouldn't have the same chthonic kind of power as those that are given.

AW: Do you throw away much work?

PM: No. It stays in the notebooks. It never gets totally thrown away. I might just get a phrase or a line or I might get a verse. I believe everything is grist to the mill. The failures are often the best part of the process, because if you can see what's gone wrong, you've learnt a huge thing. If you can see and name why it's not working then you've learnt something enormous which is impossible to teach.

AW: How do you keep energised as a poet today? Is the urge and need to write still the same as those early days?

PM: The urge is not the same, no. It's still my major daily consideration. It's a given now, everything seems to feed into this matrix of making. But I also make in other ways. I paint and make visual things, there's an interplay between the two processes. My energy is more schooled, it's more disciplined. I don't sit down at the same time every day and do writing. I find shortcuts to the place I need to be to make the poem. I've done Tai Chi for many years, which is very helpful for keeping my body energised. I'm now in my sixty-fifth year, so I'm very conscious of the ageing processes and keeping some kind of energetic system going. I walk a lot. It's embedded in my idea of metrical feet in prosody. If I'm struggling with a poem I go for a walk, putting the whole body into motion. I often come back with it sorted.

AW: How do you feel about the state of poetry today and some of the younger poets coming up?

PM: My tastes are eclectic. I spent a lot of last year reading new poetry. Mostly poets I'd never read before. I read a lot of work from transgender poets, from poets with disabilities, a lot of work by people of colour. What I was really taken by was to see poetry so identified as a site for advocacy, for championing difference, a site where issues of identity were worked out, advocated for, celebrated. Poetry can encompass all of this, it can allow people to speak for their community, especially communities that experience oppression, it can be a place where people can bring their most essential truths.

AW: What advice would you give to a younger poet today?

PM: Poetry to me is a ritualising of language to a specific end, which the poet herself, himself, or themselves may be unaware of. But we must trust the path to bring us where we need to go. So, self-validate. Do your work. Study the ones who have gone before you, who have beaten the path for you, however you find them. Follow you own instincts and your own nose, but self-validate. If you find kind people, great. I was very lucky with the community I came from: it was so under-represented and under-valued, it was considered a disadvantaged community and yet I was very conscious of the richness, of the gifts I'd been given by the people I grew up amongst. I was able to use all that loving energy to self-validate and to be self-reliant. I'd say to young poets, do not be looking to others to validate you because it's a very vulnerable position to be in. You can be taken advantage of if you relinquish your personal power. There's no HR department to bring your concerns to in our profession. So be a warrior.

AW: Finally, what does poetry do for you as a person?

PM: For me it's salvific. It's given me a path in life of enrichment beyond my dreams, in terms of friendship and the things I've made. It's been ultimately a safe path. Even though at times I think we walk on these precipices where if you look down your head would fall off. I sometimes wonder what would I be doing if I hadn't become a poet. Gardening would probably be the other safe path. I love the garden.

Notes on Contributors

Paul Batchelor was born in Northumberland, where he lives. His last chapbook was *The Love Darg* (Clutag Press, 2014). He is Director of Creative Writing at Durham University.

Natalie Linh Bolderston is a Vietnamese-Chinese-British poet. She came third in the 2019 National Poetry Competition and received an Eric Gregory Award in 2020. Her pamphlet, *The Protection of Ghosts*, is published with V. Press.

Dermot Bolger is a novelist, playwright, and poet. His fifteenth work of fiction, *Secrets Never Told*, appeared in 2020. His latest play, *Last Orders at the Dockside*, premiered at the Abbey Theatre in 2019. His *That Which is Suddenly Precious: New and Selected Poems* appeared in 2015.

Dean Browne's poems have appeared widely, including in *Banshee*, *Poetry*, *Southword*, *The Stinging Fly*, and *The Tangerine*. He was the featured poet in *The Stinging Fly* (Summer 2018), and a poem, 'Pine Box in the Flea-Market', was shortlisted for the Listowel Writers' Week Poem of the Year at The Irish Book Awards in 2019.

Scríobhann **Paddy Bushe** filíocht i nGaeilge agus i mBéarla. D'fhoilsigh Dedalus Press *Second Sight* (rogha as trí bhailiúchán a d'fhoilsigh Coiscéim, lena chuid aistriúchán féin) agus *Peripheral Vision*, bailiúchán nua Béarla, i mí Feabhra 2020. Tá cónaí air ar bhruach faille in Uíbh Ráthach, Co. Chiarraí.

Siobhán Campbell's latest book is *Heat Signature* (Seren Books, 2017). New work exploring the natural world, including birdlife, bog pools, and horses appears in *Places of Poetry* (ed. Paul Farley), *Deep Time 2* (Black Bough Press), and on the Poetry Archive's Poetry Now channel.

Liam Carson is the director of the IMRAM Irish Language Literature Festival, and the author of the memoir *call mother a lonely field*. He is currently working on *snow angels in darkness*, a poetic memoir of vivid dreaming, the 2020 pandemic, and family life. He has recently finished a collection of haiku, *the starling's wings*.

John Challis is the author of the pamphlet, *The Black Cab* (Poetry Salzburg, 2017), and is the recipient of a Pushcart Prize and a Northern Writers' Award. His first collection, *The Resurrectionists*, is due from Bloodaxe Books in 2021.

Kayo Chingonyi's debut collection, *Kumukanda* (Chatto & Windus, 2017) won the 2018 International Dylan Thomas Prize and a Somerset Maugham Award. *A Blood Condition*, a new collection of poems, will be published in 2021, also by Chatto & Windus.

Jane Clarke's second collection, *When the Tree Falls* (Bloodaxe Books, 2019), was shortlisted for The Pigott Poetry Prize 2020, *The Irish Times* Poetry Now Award 2020, and the Farmgate Café National Poetry Award 2020. She lives in Glenmalure, Co. Wicklow.

Emily S Cooper's poetry and prose are published in *The Stinging Fly*, *Banshee*, *Hotel*, and elsewhere. Her debut pamphlet, *Glass*, will be published by Makina Books in early 2021.

Ailbhe Darcy is an Irish poet living in Wales. Her most recent collection, *Insistence* (Bloodaxe Books, 2018), won Wales Book of the Year and The Pigott Poetry Prize 2019.

Katie Donovan has published five collections of poetry with Bloodaxe Books. Her most recent, *Off Duty* (2016), was shortlisted for *The Irish Times* Poetry Now Award. She received the Lawrence O'Shaughnessy Award for Irish Poetry in 2017. She lives in Dalkey, Co. Dublin.

Michael Dooley's poems have appeared in *Poetry Ireland Review*, *The Stinging Fly*, and online at RTÉ Culture. In 2020, he was shortlisted for The Strokestown International Poetry Competition, The Doolin Poetry Prize, and The Cúirt New Writing Prize. He is a teacher, and lives in Limerick.

Ian Duhig has written seven books of poetry, most recently *The Blind Roadmaker* (Picador, 2016), shortlisted for the Forward and TS Eliot Prizes. His *Selected Poems* will be published in 2021.

Maia Elsner was born in London to Mexican and Polish-Jewish parents. Her poems appear in *Magma*, *Wildness*, *Stand*, and elsewhere. She was shortlisted for the 2020 Mairtín Crawford Award for Poetry, and the 2020 Bridport Poetry Prize.

Alyson Favilla is a non-binary poet from San Diego, California, and holds an M.Phil. in Irish Writing from Trinity College Dublin. You can find their writing in *The Tangerine*, *The Honest Ulsterman*, *abridged*, and *diode*. They live and work in New York City.

Catherine Gander is a literary critic and associate professor of American literature at Maynooth University. Her writing has appeared in *The Irish Times*, *Poetry Ireland Review*, *The Guardian*, and *The Wolf*, among other publications. She is Chair of the Irish Association for American Studies.

Jonathan Greenhause won the Telluride Institute's 2020 Fischer Poetry Prize, and was on the shortlist for the 2019 Mick Imlah Poetry Prize. His poems have appeared in *Crannóg*, *The Moth*, *The Rialto*, *Southword, The Stinging Fly*, and on The Poetry Society website.

Richard Hayes is Vice President for Strategy at Waterford Institute of Technology. He has previously been Dean of the School of Humanities at the Institute, where he also lectured in English and theatre studies. He is artistic director of the Eugene O'Neill International Festival of Theatre, based in New Ross, and is a board member of GOMA, Waterford's Gallery of Modern Art.

Kathleen Jamie is one of Scotland's leading poets. Her latest collections from Picador are *The Bonniest Companie* (2015) and *Selected Poems* (2018). Her third essay collection, *Surfacing*, was published last year by Sort Of Books.

Sa Bhreatain Bheag a rugadh Diarmuid Johnson agus i gCo na Gaillimhe a tógadh é. Scríobhann sé i nGaeilge, i mBéarla agus sa Bhreatnais agus tá breis is fiche saothar foilsithe aige. Is é *Éadaoin* (Leabhar Breac, 2020) an leabhar is déanaí uaidh. Tá *Éadaoin* ar an tríú leabhar i Sraith na Teamhrach, tríológ ina ndéantar athinsint ar sheanscéalta na nGael. Tá sé ag obair sa Bhruiséil faoi láthair.

Victoria Kennefick's pamphlet, *White Whale* (Southword Editions, 2015), won the Munster Literature Centre Fool for Poetry Chapbook Competition, and the Saboteur Award for Best Poetry Pamphlet. New work features in the forthcoming *Carcanet New Poetries VIII* anthology. Her first collection will be published in 2021.

Born in Tyrone, Nick Laird is a poet, novelist, screenwriter, and former lawyer. His fourth collection, *Feel Free* (2018), was shortlisted for the TS Eliot Prize and the Derek Walcott Prize. He teaches at New York University, and at the Seamus Heaney Centre at Queen's University Belfast.

Born in Co. Durham, Martin Malone now lives in north-east Scotland. He has published three collections: *The Waiting Hillside* (Templar Poetry, 2011), *Cur* (Shoestring Press, 2015), *The Unreturning* (Shoestring Press, 2019), and *Selected Poems 2005–2020: Larksong Static* (Hedgehog Press, 2020).

Kelly Michels relocated to Ireland from the US and is currently pursuing a Ph.D. at University College Dublin. She is the author of two chapbooks, and her poems have appeared in numerous journals and magazines.

Luke Morgan's debut collection, *Honest Walls*, was published in 2016 by Arlen House. His publication credits include *Poetry Ireland Review, The Poetry Review,* the *Irish Independent,* and *Crannóg.* His second collection, *Zoo,* is forthcoming in 2021.

Julie Morrissy is an Irish poet, based in Dublin. Her debut collection *Where, the Mile End* (2019) is published by Book*hug (Canada) and tall-lighthouse (UK). She is the inaugural John Pollard Newman Fellow in Creativity at University College Dublin. She also writes about art, and is the commissioned writer for *FILE NOTE V,* forthcoming from Fire Station Artists' Studio.

File Gaeilge í **Ailbhe Ní Ghearbhuigh**. D'fhoilsigh Gallery Press cnuasach dátheangach léi dar teideal *The Coast Road* ina bhfuil aistriúcháin le filí Béarla. D'aistrigh sí féin *Dánta Andrée Chedid* ón bhFraincis (Cois Life, 2019). Bronnadh Duais Lawrence O'Shaughnessy uirthi in 2020.

Scríobhann **Doireann Ní Ghríofa** i nGaeilge agus i mBéarla. Is é *A Ghost in the Throat* (Tramp Press, 2020) an leabhar is déanaí uaithi.

Mary Noonan teaches French literature at UCC. She has published two collections with Dedalus Press: *The Fado House* (2012), and *Stone Girl* (2019). *Stone Girl* was shortlisted for the Derek Walcott Prize in 2020.

Lianne O'Hara is from Amsterdam. She writes poetry, prose, and drama. Her work has appeared in *The Honest Ulsterman, The Ogham Stone, Channel, Splonk, B O D Y, Writing Home: The 'New Irish' Poets* anthology, *Amsterdam Quarterly, Crossways,* and *Black Bough Poetry.* She lives in Dublin, where she teaches creative writing.

Taobh amuigh de shráidbhaile an Chaisleáin Nua i ndeisceart Thiobraid Árann a tógadh **Stiofán Ó hIfearnáin**. Foilsíodh filíocht dá chuid ar *Comhar, The Stinging Fly,* agus *Poetry Ireland Review.* Tá ceithre dhán leis sa duanaire dátheangach *Calling Cards* (The Gallery Press, 2018) a chuir Peter Fallon agus Aifric Mac Aodha in eagar.

James Conor Patterson is from Newry, Co. Down. His poetry has featured in *The Irish Times*, *Magma*, *New Statesman*, *Poetry Ireland Review*, *Poetry London*, *The Poetry Review*, and *The Stinging Fly*. In 2019 he was a recipient of an Eric Gregory Award.

Kate Quigley's work has been published in a number of Irish and UK journals, and their debut poetry pamphlet, *If You Love Something,* was published by Rack Press in 2019. Kate was selected as a participant in the Stinging Fly Poetry Summer School 2019, and the Poetry Ireland's Introduction Series 2020.

Denise Riley's *Selected Poems* was published in 2019 by Picador.

Felicity Sheehy's poetry appears in *The New Republic*, *The Yale Review*, *Narrative*, and elsewhere. She has received an Academy of American Poets Prize, the Jane Martin Poetry Prize, and a Tennessee Williams Scholarship to the Sewanee Writers' Conference.

Gerard Smyth's latest and tenth collection of poems, *The Sundays of Eternity*, was published by Dedalus Press in 2020.

Mary Shine Thompson's recent essay on Paula Meehan, 'Paula Meehan's Dublins: Landscape, Community and Poetic Identity', is published in *Reading Ireland: The Little Magazine* 11, Winter 2019. She edited Michael Kirby's *Skelligs Haul* (The Lilliput Press), and *Future Perfect* (Poetry Ireland and Trócaire), in 2019.

Jessica Traynor is a poet and creative writing teacher. *Liffey Swim* (Dedalus Press) was shortlisted for the Strong/Shine Award. *The Quick*, (Dedalus Press, 2018), was a 2019 *The Irish Times* poetry choice. She is Poet in Residence at the Yeats Society, Sligo, and a Creative Fellow of University College Dublin.

David Wheatley's books include *Stravaig* (Broken Sleep Books, 2021). He lives in rural Aberdeenshire.

Adam Wyeth is a poet, playwright, essayist, and creative writing teacher, with four books published with Salmon Poetry. In 2019 he received The Kavanagh Fellowship. His forthcoming collection, *about:blank* (2021), is currently in New Work development with the Abbey Theatre. Adam is an Associate Artist of the Civic Theatre, Dublin, and works on research for the RTÉ Poetry Programme.